Bud's Easy™

Research Paper Computer Manual

Seventh Edition

Alvin J. Baron, Ph. D.

Lawrence House Publishers
Larchmont, New York 10538

Bud's Easy Research Paper Computer Manual Seventh Edition

ISBN 978-1-891707-10-0

Trademarks

Published by Lawrence House Publishers
Larchmont, New York 10538

Contents

Part 2
Using Research Writing Style Books

Part 3
Writing Review

Introduction

The seventh edition of the *Research Paper Computer Manual* has been completed revised and updated. The publisher and author have renewed their commitment to provide student researchers with the best and most up to date tools.

The editors have made this edition brighter and easier to use with a fresh typeface, clearer layout, improved illustrations, and practice exercises. Content has been expanded to help researchers with the gradual shift from print to electronic sources. A full explanation of social networks, known as Web 2.0, and their use as information sources is included. The seventh edition recognizes that researchers will likely use mobile electronic devices like iPhones and Blackberrys. The new Digital Object Identifier system (DOI) which is rapidly coming into use is described.

Writing a research paper is not easy. It requires library skills, Internet skills, computer skills, and writing skills. A healthy dose of good judgement and clear thinking is also needed. The research paper is a very daunting academic hurdle and most students recoil when it is assigned.

The seventh edition endeavors to make the assignment as painless as possible by breaking it down into fifteen very manageable tasks. Each task will require some work and some time, but if you proceed in an orderly manner, the job will be accomplished with relative ease.

How To Use This Book

Read Task 1 which should clear up any misconceptions you have about research paper writing and help you get started on the right track. Take the author's advice about eliminating procrastination and organizing your time.

Most important, skim through all fifteen tasks before you begin. Get familiar with what lies ahead. When you understand that the monumental research paper assignment is really nothing but a series of very achievable smaller tasks, you will get started with enthusiasm and a sense of excitement. Do the exercises to help you learn the techniques and skills of research writing. Try to keep within the suggested times for each task. Be positive about the assignment!

Good luck with your research!

Part 1

Researching and Writing the Research Paper

Task 1

Get Started

Task 1: Get Started

Suggested Time for Task 1: 1 Hour

1.1. The Research Assignment

So you've been assigned the dreaded research paper. Admittedly, this is a daunting task. You know it will be time consuming and difficult. Writing a research paper is a scary project piled on top of all the other courses you are taking and the other personal responsibilities you have. What to do? How do you start?

First, put the job into a positive perspective. Think about it. If you do a good job on this paper, the skills you learn will prove valuable in many future school, college, and work activities. In addition, if you really handle this assignment well, your course grade may grow to an A!

Second, although writing the research paper or even the more comprehensive thesis is a challenging and demanding job, you will find that you derive much personal satisfaction when you submit a carefully crafted paper to your instructor.

Research papers are assigned because writing them will enable you to:

- Learn research skills
- Gather facts on your subject
- Develop a thesis and defend it
- Select and evaluate sources
- Improve your thinking skills
- Hone your writing skills
- Provide your sources to readers

1.2. Bud's Easy Task Method

Bud's Easy Task Method breaks the seemingly monumental assignment to write a research paper into a series of relatively simple tasks. The method provides clear instructions that make it easy to succeed. As you complete each task in sequence you will gain confidence knowing that you are moving along steadily. This book will take you through the entire process, acting as your guide along the way. Come along now and let's take the first step toward success.

> **Idea!**
> "A journey of a thousand miles begins with a single step."
> Lao-tzu, Chinese philosopher
> 604-531 B.C.

1.3. Get An Overview Of The Whole Job

Whenever you are faced with a large work assignment it is a good idea to get a picture of the entire task before you begin. Psychologists call this preparing an "Advance Organizer."

Smart students advance organize whenever they get a big, new assignment. For example, when they get their American history texts at the beginning of the term, they review the table of contents and then skim each chapter for a quick overview. They are getting the "big picture" so they will be able to see how each new event fits in the panorama of American history. This works with all subjects and tasks. It is especially important for big jobs like writing research papers.

Right now let's do an "advance organizer" to give you an overview of the job of writing a research paper and to see how all of the tasks relate to the whole project.

Open this book to the Table of Contents. Read the chapter headings. We call the chapters "Tasks" because there are a series of tasks that you have to accomplish to complete the research paper. After reading the Table of Contents, read the summary of each task in the following pages. Then open the book to that task and skim through the chapter. You will not understand all the details of each task, but you will have a better idea of the complete assignment.

When you finish this overview you will have skimmed the complete book and understand that writing a research paper is not all that difficult or complicated and you will approach the assignment with confidence.

SUMMARY OF TASKS

Task 1: Getting Started. Part of this task is getting an overview of the whole job which is what you are doing right now. You are also going to look at some problems that many students have to get moving on the assignment. You will learn how to deal with procrastination devils! Take a quick look at the rest of Task 1 in the book now.

Task 2: Develop a Thesis Question. This task begins with finding a good topic to write about. You will be given suggestions for locating a great topic that really interests you. Once that is decided you will learn how to formulate a challenging Thesis Question about your topic. For example, if you are interested in education, a good Thesis Question would be: How is public school achievement related to socioeconomic class? Or if you are inclined toward world politics, this would be interesting: Why should the United States negotiate with known terrorist organizations? Skim through Task 2 in the book.

Task 3: Learn To Evaluate Sources. Once you have nailed down your Thesis Question you will be interested in finding the answer by looking in the library for books and magazines and in Web sites. But before you go off, you must have an important tool in your research paper tool chest. You must develop a skill set for evaluating sources. Task 3 will train you to be an astute and careful researcher who can quickly judge the qualtity of any book, article, or Web site. Take a quick look at Task 3 in the book for a few details.

Task 4: Learn To Set Up A Bibliography File. At this point in the project you have learned to tell right from wrong when you search. But before you go to the library or the Internet you must add another tool to your chest. You must learn how to set up a system to keep track of all the good sources you find by building a Bibliography file in your computer. When you get to the library or Internet you will use this tool to record all the important bibliographic data such as authors' names, titles, and any other important information. Quickly check out the exercises that teach you how to do this by skimming Task 4 in the book now.

Task 5: Learn to Set Up A Note File. Here's another important tool. This task will teach you how to build a computer Note file. When you find good material in a book, magazine, or Web site, you must put it into your Note file as a direct quote, a summary, or a paraphrase. This takes a bit of practice. Of course, your Note file will be linked to your Bibliography file. Scan Task 5 now. Don't bother about the details, just get the idea.

Task 6: Search The Physical Library. Finally, armed with the tools of evaluation, Bibliography files, and Note files, you are ready to begin your research. Task 6 will be a foray into the library where you will meet the media specialist who will help you in your search for answers to your Thesis Question. You will learn a lot about the various library collections and how to use the online catalog. When you are finished in the library, you should have a small batch of Bibliography and Note files from sources about your Thesis Question. Flip through the pages of Task 6 now to see what is involved.

Task 7: Search The Internet. When you finish searching the library for sources, you will learn in this task how to attack the Internet to locate a few more good sources. In your quest to answer your Thesis Question, you will add any new material you find to your Bibliography and Note files. Skim through Task 7 to learn how good Internet searching will be done.

Task 8: Search Databases. This task takes you to the library's online catalog where you will learn to explore sources in all kinds of electronic databases. Again, you will add to your cache of Bibliography and Note files. You may not know much about databases, but cast your eyes over Task 8 now to get some ideas.

Task 9: Prepare Your Thesis Statement. By now you will have largely completed your research. You will have absorbed much information and come to some conclusions about your Thesis Question and developed a positive position about it. You will learn how to turn your Thesis Question into your Thesis Statement. Read Task 9 quickly to see how you can change your Question into a Statement.

Task 10: Prepare Your Outline. Here is another tool for your chest. You will learn how to prepare an outline with a series of topics and sub-topics in an Outline file in your computer. The outline will be the framework for your research paper that will prove your Thesis Statement. Task 10 is pretty simple. Give it a short look.

Task 11: Flesh Out Your Outline. Here you will put some meat on the outline's bones with the research you've done. You will learn how to transfer material from your Note file directly into your Outline file. This is a mechanical job, so peruse Task 11 to see what is involved.

Task 12 The Writing Process. In this task you will learn how to build great, powerful paragraphs and to tie them together in a well-written paper. This chapter is instructional. You will be learning how to improve your writing style. Read Task 12 quickly to get an inkling of what you are going to learn.

Tasks 13, 14, and 15. Write Three Drafts. In Task 13 you will transfer material from your Outline file to the first draft and you will learn how to cite sources in your paper. When you write Draft 2 in Task 14, you will carefully proofread for possible plagiarism, citation errors, and proper development of your ideas. Finally, in Task 15 you will prepare your final draft by adding the bibliography, title page, and by making a final check of spelling and grammar. Your work will be done! Quickly scan these three chapters for an overview of the final work.

You now have your "Advance Organizer" in your head. Let's go to work! You have the big picture and will not be surprised by a part of the assignment you did not expect. As you complete each task you will see how the parts "fit" together to make up the whole.

Getting Started - The First Step

It may seem obvious that you have to get started on this research project. It may even seem unusual that there is a need to discuss how to get started. Unfortunately, many students find that getting started is the most difficult part of writing a research paper. Because they fail to get going soon enough, some do not do their best in this academic exercise. They just can't get going soon enough, and then fail to do well under time pressure.

This task is simply to get moving. But getting started is not always as easy as it seems. Many people delay the start of difficult tasks. This is called procrastination. The causes are varied, but the result is most often negative. It's true that procrastination will shorten the time you have to be involved with the writing of the paper, but it ultimately creates stress and anxiety, things we can certainly do without. Procrastination is an unhealthful way of dealing with a job you don't like. So what makes us delay? Some of the causes may surprise you.

1.4. The Six Procrastination Devils

1.4.1. Fear of Failure

Some students don't feel smart enough or capable enough to write a research paper. They are afraid they will be embarrassed in front of friends and teachers if they do the paper poorly. Such students delay the start. With insufficient time to write, they submit a weak paper. Then to save face for themselves and their friends, they invent excuses for their procrastination. They say, "I got started late because I had too many other assignments." or "If I had given it more time, I would have gotten at least a B+." Procrastination is a way out for these students.

1.4.2. Fear of Success

Strange as it sounds, this is the other side of the coin. Some students subconsciously fear that if they write a terrific paper and get an A they might not be able to maintain such a high standard. If they don't keep the A's coming, they are afraid everyone may discover that they are really not so smart. They think, "Maybe it is better not to try at all." These students just procrastinate until they don't have to prove anything about their brain power.

1.4.3. Perfectionism

The perfectionistic students feel they must always excel. They spend inordinate amounts of time on tasks that usually turn out very well done, but the pressure to be perfect often prevents these students from initiating or completing tasks. They procrastinate because it is just too hard to be perfect all the time.

1.4.4. Pleasure Seeking

Pleasure seekers are very common in schools and colleges. These students like dating, texting, YouTubing, Facebooking, and sleeping late. They frequently feel bored by school work and dislike their courses and teachers. They find tests unreasonably difficult as if the teachers intentionally make them so. They rebel against teachers who expect them to do decent work. Faced with all these intrusions on their pleasures, these students procrastinate.

1.4.5. Insufficient Skills

Some students come to the realization that they are not prepared to write a real research paper. Perhaps they never learned the necessary research or writing skills. Students with these shortcomings don't know where or how to begin. They waste time nervously delaying the inevitable when they will have to reveal their deficiencies. Result: Procrastination.

1.4.6. Task Enormity

There are those who look at the research paper assignment and see it as a task so enormous that they are paralyzed by its sheer size. They may never have faced a problem so large and all encompassing. They do not see that the research paper, as is true of most difficult assignments, is really a collection of smaller jobs. Each of these tasks is significantly less daunting than the whole and much more easily completed. Nevertheless, the easy way out is to procrastinate.

1.5. Get Rid Of The Procrastination Devils.

First, do a little self-examination. Ask yourself, honestly, if you are a victim of one of the procrastination devils. If the answer is no, you are probably not being frank. Almost all human beings, because we are so human, exhibit one or more of these procrastination traits. If you are lucky enough not to suffer from the procrastination devils, you can skip the next few paragraphs. But if you are like the other ninety-nine percent of us, read on to find ways to get yourself out of procrastination modes.

1.5.1. Rid Yourself of Fear of Failure, Fear of Success, and Perfectionism

Talk to yourself. So you're afraid you'll flunk. You're going to look stupid in front of friends and teachers. You're fearful that if you do a good job, you won't be able to maintain that high standard. You're beating yourself up because of the effort it will take to do a perfect paper.

OK, you've admitted to being bothered by fear of failure, fear of success, or perfectionism. So how can you get rid of these procrastination devils?

Here's How to Do It!

1. Get real! Only a few get really top grades all the time. You don't have to get an A+.
2. No one demands that you be Mr. or Ms. Perfect. Perfect people who have no blemishes can be dull. Everyone has different strengths and weaknesses. A good paper, created through honest effort, will be good enough.
3. If you earn a B for this paper and get only a B for the course, you are in the top quarter or top third of the class, so you will still be maintaining yourself as a very good student.

1.5.2. Rid Yourself of the Need for Pleasure Seeking

You're the hedonist in the class. You like your pleasures and are not crazy about school work. You are not alone. So, let's get a few things straight in order to get yourself started.

Here's How To Do It!

1. Work is not always fun. Be mature in your outlook.
2. Writing a research paper is a reasonable project, not a hateful assignment by a mean teacher.
3. Change your attitude from "I really don't like this." to "I might get something good out of this assignment."
4. Avoid your pleasurable activities when you are working.
5. Reward yourself with something you enjoy AFTER you have completed part of a task. For example, treat yourself to an ice cream. Schedule your work around favorite TV shows. Turn them on only if you have finished a job part. Return to your tasks after the reward.

1.5.3. Rid Yourself of the Goblin of Task Enormity

You're absolutely correct. Writing a research paper is a big, big job, probably the biggest task you've ever been given in school. So what can be done?

Here's How To Do It!

1. Break the job into small segments.
2. Work on each task only 30 minutes at a time at first.
3. Start and stop several times each day to help you get into the habit of working on the project.
4. Make a written schedule. Write: "I will start Task 2 at 8:30 AM and stop at 9:00."
5. Get in the habit of making "To Do" lists daily and weekly in which you detail all of your assignments, including those involving the research paper.

1.5.4. Get Rid of Insufficient Skill Insecurity

If this is the first time you've done a research paper, it's understandable that you are a bit unsure of yourself. But remember, if you've gotten this far in school, you likely have most of the necessary skills to do the tasks required. If you are deficient in one or more skills, don't despair or give up. This book will provide the help you need!

Here's How To Do It!

1. Listen carefully to your teacher's instructions as he or she outlines the things that have to be done at each phase of each task.
2. Read and follow the instructions in this book. They are designed to break down the tasks into easy to understand procedures.
3. Identify any areas of skill weakness. Be honest. Spelling, punctuation, and usage frequently need help. So do computer skills. Read Part 2 Grammar, Mechanics, and Usage Review of this book that has all the information you need to help with those areas. Then ask friends or teachers for help with other concerns.

This book is designed to help you complete an A+ paper.

The assignment has been broken down into clearly defined tasks.

Detailed instructions will guide you through the completion of each task.

As you finish each task, you will have a sense of accomplishment, knowing that you are moving ahead with all deliberate speed and confidence.

Task 2

Develop A Thesis Question

Task 2: Develop A Thesis Question

Suggested Time for Task 2: 1-3 Hours

2.1. Topic Selection

Before developing a Thesis Question, you must first decide on a topic. Your instructor may assign one or you may be free to select a subject. If the choice is yours, select a topic that really interests you. If you are having trouble settling on a topic, you can use one of the search engine directories to scan through loads of potential topics to find one of interest.

Here's how to do it:

2.1.1 Use Search Engine Directories

Just below you will see Google's directory that you can reach by clicking on **directory Google.com.**

Run through the topics to find an area of your interest.

Illustration 2.1. Google Directory

Suppose you have concerns about the problems facing society.

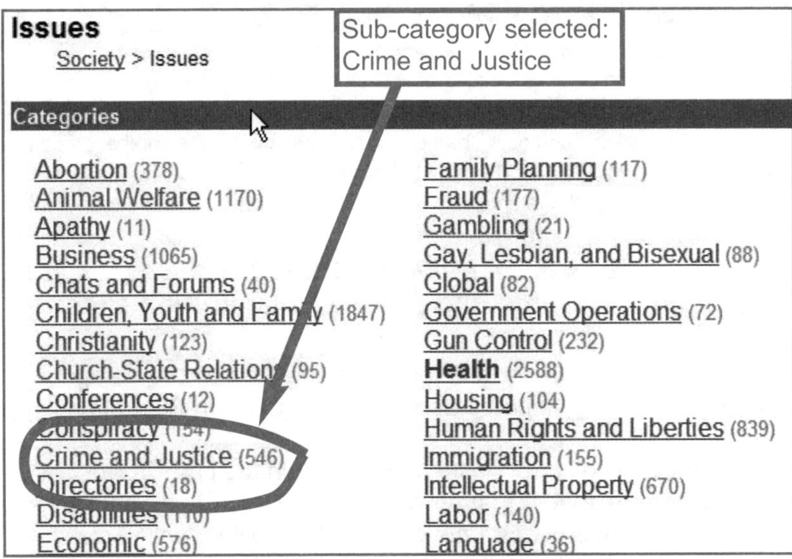

Illustration 2.2. Google Categories: Issues in Society

A click on the **Issues** link under **Society** will bring up a list of **Issues** as shown above in Illustration 2.2. As you peruse the list of sub-categories under **Issues**, you may find that **Crime and Justice** is an area that you have thought about. Clicking on that issue will bring up a page like the one below in Illustration 2.3.

Illustration 2.3. More Crime and Justice Categories

Web Pages — Viewing in Google Pag

United States Department of Justice - http://www.usdoj.gov/
Primary federal criminal investigation and enforcement agency.

Transparency International (TI) - http://www.transparency.org/
International non-governmental organisation devoted to combating corrup

National Criminal Justice Reference Service - http://www.ncjrs.
Lists publications and links on corrections, courts, crime, drugs, interna

HomeFair.com - http://www.homefair.com/early97/crime/crimelab.htn
Compares crime rates for major North American cities.

Illustration 2.4. Crime and Justice Related Web sites

In addition, a list of Web Pages related to the category of **Crime and Justice** appears as shown just above in Illustration 2.4.

As you look through the categories on the page in Illustration 2.3. you realize that **injustice** is something you've been thinking about. You wonder what a click on that link will reveal. Four categories of injustice plus a list of web pages related to **injustice** will come up as shown below in Illustration 2.5.

You could delve further looking at the additional category of **institutional Injustice** or you could begin browsing the web pages looking for more ideas for a topic.

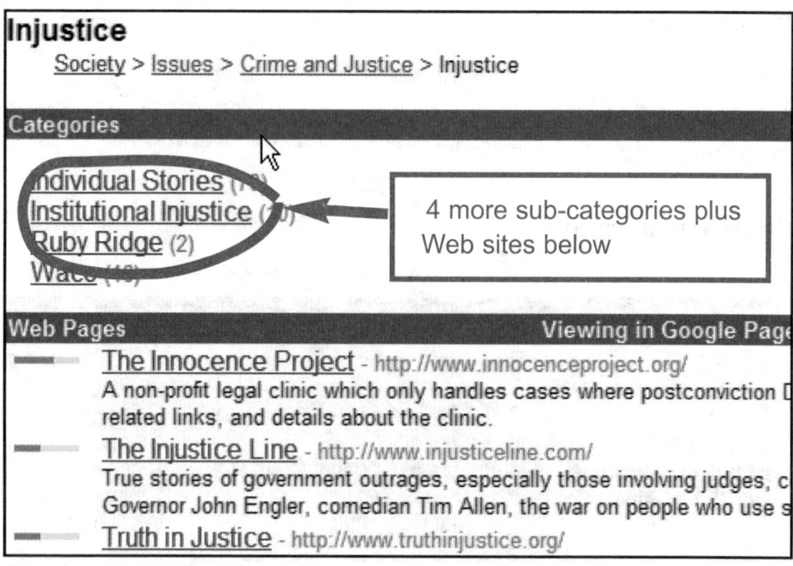

Illustration 2.5. More Categories and Web Pages

Search engine directories are powerful tools to help you home in on a suitable topic. Most search engines provide directories similar to Google's. Here are some you may want to try.

Yahoo!Directory
About.com
Internet Public Library
WWW.Virtual Library

2.1.2. Use Physical Library Resources

Don't neglect the resources of your physical school or community library. Trained personnel will direct you to the many print and non-print resources available for a topic search.

1. Ask your media specialist for help.
2. Check tables of contents and indexes of books.
3. Look through newspapers and magazines.
4. Skim encyclopedias, journals, and abstracts.

Develop Thesis Question

2.2. Thesis Question

Once you have decided on a topic, your goal is to develop an interesting preliminary Thesis Question about that topic. As you go through search engine directories and other sources, think of challenging, probing questions about the topic. Here are a series of techniques that will help you focus on a particular question about your topic.

2.2.1 Use Pre-Writing

Most good writers use several techniques of pre-writing before they begin to put their ideas on paper. Pre-writing is an important part of the writing process that can help you reflect on and connect with your subject. Here are some helpful pre-writing exercises.

Start a Scrapbook

1. Collect clippings of newspaper, magazine, and web articles. Watch TV programs.
2. Jot down idea and issues.
3. Do you have questions about any of the issues?

Free Write

1. Open a blank page in your computer or use your notebook. Write without interruption for ten minutes letting all the ideas about your topic spill out on the page. This is for your eyes only, so write without concern for grammar, spelling or punctuation. Let the ideas flow.
2. Review what you have written. Can you begin to see some organization in the ideas you have generated?
3. Rephrase your ideas as questions that you think you can answer with research. Are you getting excited about wanting to find answers to your questions? Have you begun to zero in on a Thesis Question?

Brainstorm

Brainstorming is a technique for generating lots of ideas without anyone saying, “Oh, that’s stupid!” or “That doesn’t make sense.” The purpose is to get as many ideas out as possible with no negative thoughts or comments. That will come later when you have all the ideas on paper and arranged in some order. Then you can evaluate, but not before.

1. Jot down as many questions or ideas about your topic as fast as they come to you for ten minutes.
2. Analyze your brainstormed lists. Is there one area that seems attractive to you? Are certain ideas related? Can you begin to narrow your thoughts into a “how” or “why” question?

Diagram or Map

Use this technique to find the major topics and sub-topics of your possible Thesis Question by arranging them in a graphic format.

1. Use a clean sheet of paper or white board and markers.
2. Write the topic in the center of the board or page.
3. Working rapidly, write as many ideas about your topic spreading them around the page or board.
4. When all of your ideas are out, look for terms or ideas that are related. Is one a cause of the other or an effect of the other? Is one term an example of another?

5. Draw an oval around each idea and join the ideas with lines to show the relationship among them.
6. You might use different colored markers to show the various relationships. For example, you might use a blue line to join examples of a topic, a red to join comparisons, a green to join contrasts, a yellow to join causes and effects, etc.
7. When you finish you should see the clustering of ideas in a colorful diagram or map.
8. Study the map and look for questions you might want to research.

Use the Journalist's Six Questions: 5W's and How

Prepare to answer the questions: Who? What? When? Where? Why? and How? Journalists are trained to answer these questions as they write their news stories, usually highlighting the question that is most important to their story.

Write a question about your topic beginning with each of the words Who, What, When, Where, Why, and How.

The most challenging are the How and Why questions. The Who, What, When, Where questions are less so because they can usually be answered by simple research. Nevertheless, the information in those questions can provide valuable background for the better How and Why questions.

Is there one question that you find particularly interesting?

2.2.2. Draft Your Thesis Question

After reading articles you found using Web Directories and Library Resources and after doing the Pre-Writing Activities, you should have some ideas for thesis questions that are interesting, probing, and challenging.

Ask yourself questions about your topic. If you can pose a significant question about an important subject, you are on your way to developing a Thesis Question. Your research will attempt to find the answers to your question.

For example, if you were stirred by the issues of injustice in the criminal justice system, the following question might have occurred to you:

Why does it takes so long for some prisoners to prove that they are, in fact, innocent when solid evidence exists?

This is a good Thesis Question because it will stimulate thinking in others. Your readers may ask: How many prisoners are trying to prove their innocence? Why were they convicted? Are there faults in the types of evidence currently used? Is race an issue in convictions?

Or, suppose you were interested in Internet social networks such as Facebook and MySpace. You did some pre-writing brainstorming and generated the following random ideas:

Types of social networks: religious, social, business, school;
Origins of social networks
Effects on individuals
Why are networks popular?
Impact on daily life
Privacy concerns

After reviewing your brainstorming output, you might pose the following Thesis Question:

How will Internet based social networks like Facebook and MySpace affect society in the next ten years?

This is an excellent thesis question because your research may lead others to compare Internet social networking with older more traditional forms of networking. Or your readers may wonder what the effect of the loss of privacy will be among users.

Or perhaps you are interested in comparing the Great Depression with the economic crisis of 2008-2009. You read newspapers, prepared a scrap book, and did some free-writing. You elicited several ideas such as:

Causes of the two crises
Regulation vs. deregulation
Unemployment
Effect on families
Economic warning signals
Greed as economic motive

You think about all of the ideas you generated and the following Thesis Question might come to mind:

Why did economists not react to economic warning signals?

This is a good Thesis Question because it might lead your readers to ask what warning signals were apparent in past economic panics?

As you can see the best Thesis Questions are **How** and **Why** questions. The **Who, What, When**, and **Where** questions usually generate fairly simplistic answers that may not be stimulating to your readers.

2.2.3. Refine Your Thesis Question

Your job as a researcher is to get all the information you can that will answer your Thesis Question. You haven't done any serious research yet, so don't be surprised if you decide to shift your focus as you delve into your subject.

Later on in this project, after you have carefully accumulated data on your subject you will develop a Thesis Statement from your Thesis Question. This statement will be in declarative form and your research paper will "prove" your Thesis Statement.

For now you must narrow your Thesis Question into one that is manageable. Don't try to tackle a subject that is too broad for a class research paper. On the other hand, don't be a nitpicker and select a very narrow subject.

Ask yourself, "Will this be of interest to my audience?" Am I excited about pursuing this subject with enthusiasm?' Be certain that your proposed topic is scholarly enough for serious research. Frivolous subjects have no place in school research.

Study the Thesis Question Checklist that follows. Keep working on your Thesis Question until it passes all the checklist criteria. Share your ideas with classmates. Ask your library media specialist for his or her opinion. Discuss your proposed topic with your teacher.

THESIS QUESTION CHECKLIST

▶ **Not too broad**	"How have current tax policies affected the economy?" **not** "How have tax policies changed in the U.S. over the past 200 years?"
▶ **Not too narrow**	"How has NAFTA affected trade with Mexico?" **not** "How do banana imports from Mexico compare with banana imports from Brazil?"
▶ **Interesting to readers**	"Why is solar energy a better alternate fuel than wind power?" **not the obvious** "Should we seek other fuels?"
▶ **Not too technical**	"How do blueberries affect the aging process?" **not** "How does hippocampal plasticity affect memory?" (Unless OK with your instructor!)
▶ **Scholarly**	"How did slavery in New York State just prior to the Civil War influence political parties?" **not** "How does gossip about movie stars affect their popularity?"
▶ **Interesting to you**	Opens a new, challenging area to you.
▶ **OK with Instructor**	Meets subject, length, or other criteria.

My Thesis Question Is:

Task 3

Learn To Evaluate Sources

Task 3: Learn To Evaluate Sources

Suggested Time for Task 3: 1 Hour

3.1. Develop A Research Mindset

Before you begin to research your Thesis Question it is important that you develop a critical mindset. As a researcher, you are not reading for pleasure as you would a mystery novel. Your reading has a very specific task. You are on a quest to locate credible information on your selected Thesis Question. This means that you have to become very discriminating as you read, differentiating between simplistic, inconsequential information and significant, carefully documented data. In this section you will learn how to select the worthwhile and reject the unqualified sources. But first, let's examine a problem that plagues many researchers: understanding the difference between fact and opinion.

3.1.1. Fact vs. Opinion

One of the difficulties in researching and writing is differentiating between fact and opinion. Information that is presented as fact may actually be an opinion. Frequently, even the most highly educated among us confuse the two. So let's see what the difference is.

The American Heritage College Dictionary, Fourth Edition offers these definitions:

Opinion

"1. A belief or conclusion held with confidence but not substantiated by positive knowledge or proof.
2. A judgment based on special knowledge and given by an expert."

Fact

"1. Knowledge or information based on real occurrences.
2a. Something demonstrated to exist or known to have existed.
2b. A real occurrence or event."

The trouble is that facts can be as slippery as opinions. Wasn't it a "fact" that the earth was the center of the universe before

Galileo proved otherwise? Wasn't it a "fact" that beginning with ancient civilizations and until the 19th century bleeding of seriously ill patients was considered a satisfactory treatment. Well into the 20th century no less than a Harvard anthropologist proved with "facts" that there was a relationship between race and criminality. Even on the current issue of global warming there are scientists who have the "facts" to prove that it is or is not occurring.

It is perfectly OK to use the opinions of your sources as long as you report them as such. The opinions of experts with real credentials are fine in a research paper. As you begin your research you may discover that there are strong opinions pro and con on your Thesis Question and all seemingly based on "facts" that the writers believe to be true.

Nonetheless, do your best to be certain that the facts you report are actually facts. Test the statements of facts by squaring them against the definitions above. Try to determine that the facts have been corroborated by others who are expert in the area.

Above all, don't be afraid to question the accuracy of facts and the quality of the opinions of those writers whom you plan to include in your paper. One of the hallmarks of good research is fact checking. All good newspapers and publishers fact check to be sure that everything they print is as accurate as possible.

3.2. Evaluating Print Sources

Now let's get to the task of evaluating sources. How will you know that a source is really good? How can you identify and reject those unworthy of use in your research? Which sources are the best? The following information will give you some standards to apply. When you finish studying this section you will be better prepared to begin your search in print sources.

3.2.1. Primary Print Sources

Primary sources are original documents. Examples are letters; census data; legal documents; court decisions; charts; maps; statistical data; literary works such as poems, novels, and plays; works of art; musical compositions; and some news stories. You are free to express your own ideas about these sources as if you are the first to see or read them. For example, you can state your own opinion about a poem or a legal decision.

3.2.2. Secondary Print Sources

These are the articles, commentaries, reviews, and editorials that discuss the primary sources. For example, a bill of sale for a slave bought or sold in 1791 is a primary source. Comments that you find about that sale in later writings are considered secondary sources.

Secondary sources require careful scrutiny. It is among these sources that you must make the important decisions about quality. The following criteria should be used in making your judgement.

RECENCY

It makes sense to use secondary sources that are the most recent. Ideas about major issues change as new information becomes available. If you are writing about space exploration, it is obvious that you need to find the most recent articles and books about the subject. Therefore, as you search, you should be looking for the latest possible copyright dates.

An exception to the recency check occurs if you are writing an historical review of the topic or if older material is relevant. For example, if you plan to show how advances in the treatment of an illness occurred over time, it would be appropriate to include information found in an older scientific journal.

AUTHOR'S REPUTATION AND BACKGROUND

The author of a source may be a person, organization, or committee. If the author or authors are persons, you must be sure they are truly qualified to write about the subject. She or he must be well-known and should hold academic degrees in the field or have years of experience. There should be affiliations with institutions of high caliber such as universities or governmental agencies.

The author should be reasonably prolific with articles published in academic journals or high quality magazines such as *Scientific American* but not *Popular Mechanics* or the *Ladies Home Journal.* Virtually every conceivable area of study has at least one and in some cases dozens of journals that publish scholarly articles with the latest research. Some journals are "peer reviewed" which means that scholars from the same field evaluate articles before they are accepted for publication.

The author's work should be scholarly and detailed, reflecting careful research. The author's sources should be available in footnotes, endnotes, and/or bibliographies. These notes may lead you to additional sources for your own work and will allow you to see how the author reached his or her conclusions.

Avoid articles in any sensational books or magazines. The *Enquirer* and *The Star* should definitely not be on your list of potential sources unless you are examining the impact of such sources on society or are exploring the genre.

TIP

Today you can do a quick check of an author's background by typing "Biography of and author's name" in a Google search box. You should get a pretty good idea of your source's credentials and background. Look for comments about the author from a variety of sources.

RELEVANCE

You will undoubtedly find several articles on your topic. Some may seem related at first, but take a close look to be sure you are keeping within the limits of your subject. For example, if you were writing about a specific cure for diabetes, you might find an article that discusses all of the current approaches. Better to locate articles that zero in on the specific treatment you want to write about.

OBJECTIVITY AND BIAS

Almost every article or book you read will carry some bias, either intentional or unintentional. Writers cannot totally eliminate the bias in their writings even if they try because they live in a stew of social, political, economic, scientific and historical influences. Even physical scientists who strive for objectivity occasionally fail to recognize that bias in favor of their hypotheses has crept into their research.

So bias exists. Therefore, you should carefully vet each source to determine the degree of bias. If you suspect or know that some bias is present, you may still find the source valuable and use it in your paper. However, you should comment on your perception of the author's slant on the topic.

Bias in Newspapers and Magazines

The professional training of journalists stresses the ethical standards of objectivity and fairness in reporting. For the most part, journalists strive to adhere to those ethical guidelines. Journalists really try to write stories that are complete, objective, and fair. Yet, inevitably, some bias may seep into the stories that appear in our daily newspapers and magazines.

Many newspapers and general interest magazines are known to be either liberal or conservative. Writers who work for a liberal or conservative publication may use language, sometimes unintentionally, that carries the message the publisher wants to convey. You should be aware, as you search, of the political leaning of any publications you use.

Remember too, that newspapers and magazines are in business to make money. Therefore, these publications may be under pressure to avoid stories with negative information about their advertisers or conversely to print stories that promote products.

Bias in Organization and Business Communication

Assume that the publications of organizations and businesses will favor and support their goals and actions. The Sierra Club, an environmental activist organization, will certainly disagree with major oil companies about the effects of drilling on the environment. Will labor unions and businesses line up on the same side of major issues? Not likely. Pharmaceutical companies have been known to sponsor scientific research studies that support the effectiveness of their drugs. You, as an astute researcher, should be sensitive to the possibility of bias in statements from organizations and businesses.

TIP

Check an organization's history and mission by going to its website and clicking on its "About Us" tab. Of course, the information will be written by the organization itself, so it may be slanted. More checking should be done with a Google search.

Bias in Government Communications

Governmental agencies sometimes issue statements that reflect the position of the party that is in power. Elected officials - and most are honorable public servants - naturally try to persuade listeners and readers to support their point of view. Who is correct about the national debt? Is it too high or just fine? Should we allow mining in federal wilderness areas or should they be forever wild? As you can see, simple answers to these questions are not easy to come by.

You should absolutely assume that foreign governments make pronouncements of policy that will be in that government's interest.

ACTION

Identifying Bias

Ask the following questions:

1. What are the author's political or social affiliations?
2. Who is paying for the information or supporting it?
3. Does the newpaper, magazine, journal, blog, or web page have a known political or social bias?
4. What are the author's sources?
5. If the author cites statistics, who compiled them? How and when were they compiled?
6. Are other points of view included or not?
7. Are positive words used for the author's point of view? Are negative words used to describe the alternative view?

ACCURACY

Most readers have difficulty determining whether a particular statement is accurate or not. You should be able to rely on trustworthy writers to report factually on ideas or events. However, try to corroborate information by checking several sources.

How does inaccurate information get published? Newspaper stories are usually written quickly to meet deadlines so even the best intentioned editing may miss errors. Major news gathering agencies go to great lengths to do "fact checking" before allowing stories to be published. Still, errors creep into many news articles.

Several years ago even the prestigious *New York Times* fired a reporter who had plagiarized or invented stories and had them approved by editors. Several of his supervising editors left as well. In 2004 the *Times* issued a major statement admitting that some its news stories about the Iraq war had been inaccurate. Subsequently, the newspaper established more stringent rules for insuring the accuracy of reporters' stories.

Misinformation

Misinformation is information that is simply incorrect or inaccurate that is promulgated intentionally or accidentally. For example, articles describing the benefits of certain herbs as cures for diseases can be misleading and based on faulty science. Sometimes reporters simply get the facts wrong. During the Katrina hurricane in Louisiana in 2005 there were early reports of crimes and deaths that later turned out to be exaggerated. Unfortunately, researchers like yourself may use erroneous information believing that the source is credible.

Newspapers regularly publish corrections when errors are brought to their attention, but these usually follow the original stories by several days and are generally buried in small print on inside pages. Consequently, corrections frequently go unnoticed by readers and researchers.

Disinformation

Disinformation is data that is falsified intentionally. At times, especially during wars, a country may attempt to confuse its enemy or encourage support for its cause by disseminating disinformation about battles or strategies. Be aware of the possibility that a propaganda office may have generated false information.

In sum, each source should be screened for recency, author's reputation, scholarship, relevance, bias and accuracy. Use the Source Quality Checklist shown below to check the quality of every print source you use.

Eliminate any sources that fall short in any of the criteria and retain only those you can be sure will increase the value of your paper.

Print Source Evaluation Checklist	
▶ Primary Sources:	First hand material such as letters, documents, novels, news stories, original web pages. Excellent material.
▶ Secondary Sources:.......	Material written about primary sources, events, or ideas.
▶ Recency....................	Most recent unless historically significant.
▶ Author's reputation....	Well-known in field, prolific, university scholar.
▶ Scholarship...............	Material footnoted, detailed, accurate. Extensive, scholarly sources. No sensational, "low-brow" magazines.
▶ Relevance...............	Relates closely to topic.
▶ Objectivity................	Clear point of view. Recognizes ideas of others. Relatively bias free.
▶ Accuracy..................	Facts corroborated with other sources.

3.3. Evaluating Internet Sources

3.3.1. The Internet in Perspective

Scholars are still studying the ways that the invention of the printing press changed civilization. In the 15th century Johann Gutenberg invented movable type and printed the Bible. For the first time information could be rapidly disseminated to the masses. The press revolutionized thinking and is credited with fomenting the Protestant Reformation of Martin Luther as well as fostering the intellectual explosion of the Renaissance.

If the printing press was such a tremendous force that it could stimulate enormous changes in the ways people thought about the world, religious relationships, scientific inquiry, art, government, and a host of other issues, it is difficult to imagine the impact the Internet will have on humankind in the future. When the sixth edition of this manual was written in 2007, we predicted that the Internet would prove to be manyfold more powerful than the printing press.

The Internet vs. Print Media

Obviously, we were prescient. Today information on any subject is available to anyone with a computer. From your computer or mobile device you can access data from millions of websites and thousands of libraries. Cell phones, iPhones, and other mobile devices loaded with "apps" offer instantaneous communication plus loads of information. iPods can be used to access the Internet and download data that can later be transferred to your computer.

Google plans to digitize every book ever printed and make them available on the Web. Many standard reference works are on the Internet and revised frequently providing updated information not possible with annual print publications. Primary sources in far away libraries may now be accessed easily. The problem for the Internet researcher is the plethora of information. There is just too much and it is hard to filter.

Traditionally, newspapers have been the primary source of daily news. Minutes after the latest edition goes to press, there is breaking news that newspapers will not have, so radio and television provide up to the minute news coverage 24/7. But today the Internet has largely usurped the roles of newspapers, radio, and television and reshaped the way we communicate and get information.

Most young people depend on the Internet for news and do not read daily newspapers. Newspapers, the traditional print media, are facing loss of readership and advertising revenue and are rapidly disappearing. Traditionally, newspaper journalists have served as the watchdogs of society, reporting on government, investigating businesses, and uncovering scandals through rigorous investigation; but maintaining news rooms and news bureaus around the world is proving too costly for newspapers. Will the sponsors of Web sites provide the watchdog function of old-fashioned print media? Can Internet viewers and listeners be assured of the same standards of fact checking and editing?

3.3.2. Impact of Web 2.0 Social Media

As if the World Wide Web hadn't created enough change, Web 2.0 with YouTube, Facebook, and all the social networks is adding yet another dimension to the way we communicate in the ether.

Social networks like Facebook, MySpace, and LinkedIn; personal, group, corporation, organizational and media blogs; micro-blogs such as Twitter; social bookmarking programs such as Digg, Reddit, Delicious, and StumbleUpon; knowledge sharing sites such as Wikipedia, and the photo and video sharing of YouTube and Flickr are having a tremendous impact on the dissemination of information.

News reporting has been turned on its head. Instead of professional journalists finding and reporting the news to the world, the people at large are creating the news. A democratic shift has occurred because one no longer has to have enough money to own a newspaper, publish a magazine, or even just buy a printing press to publish. Anyone can generate and manipulate stories.

However, with this shift, the rigorous constraints of editing, fact checking, and deciding what to print are no longer in place. *The New York Times* still carries its motto on its front page, "All the News That's Fit To Print," but few in the blogosphere adhere to that principle. Unfortunately, many Internet stories are false or inaccurate and are sped around the globe at the speed of light. Sadly, most people believe that if a story appears on the Internet it is true!

The power of this democratic journalism - this bottom up dissemination of stories - is stupendous. Compared with the impact of a news story or editiorial in a national newspaper, an exciting piece whirling around in Web 2.0 wins hands down!

Totalitarian governments fear these new forms of communication and they often shut down or censor the Web, social networks, and text messaging. However, during the protests after the Iranian election of 2009, CNN reported that many of the young demonstrators used these technologies as a tool to coordinate their protests over the election's outcome. Protesters also posted graphic pictures and videos of the crackdown by officials. It is believed that they used Twitter to call people to march and to spread the word about clashes with police, despite efforts by authorities to block news of the protests.

No doubt the Internet, blogs, YouTube, and cell phone text messaging are having a tremendous effect on political and social institutions throughout the world. However, because Internet sources lack editorial controls, most Web sites and all Web 2.0 sites must be subjected to rigorous evaluation. Many communications are sent with Web "tags" that do not reveal the true identity of the sender so you cannot know anything of the author's reputation. Text messages, Tweets, and Facebook comments can be totally misleading. Although CNN and the major television news outlets aired the Tweets and camera pictures from Iran in 2009, they were careful to remind viewers that they could not be responsible for the accuracy of their sources.

Armed with a camera and some Photoshop software, people can invent situations that are completely false. During the Israeli invasion of Lebanon in 2006 several media journalists on site reported that they had seen intentionally distorted coverage of the events in favor of Hezbollah, including false or misleading captions on photographs. Some photographs submitted to Reuters and the Associated Press showed the same Lebanese woman mourning on two different pictures by two photographers, allegedly taken two weeks apart. One photographer had 900 of his photos withdrawn by the Reuters news agency when he admitted that he had altered photographs of an attack on Beirut.

3.3.3. Use Caution With Web Sources

Understand that print sources can be just as suspect as those on the Web, but given the quantity and variety of what appears on the Web, it is easy to be fooled. You must be alert to the danger of using inappropriate or inaccurate sources. You must apply the same rigorous standards to evaluate Web sources that you do for your print sources.

If you restrict your Internet search to academic journals, magazines in databases, well-known sources previously in print, government publications, and standard reference works, you should have few concerns. However, use caution with material in Web 2.0 and do not allow yourself to be fooled by Internet pitfalls.

The issues of recency, author's reputation, relevance, bias, accuracy, misinformation, and disinformation are as paramount in evaluting Web sources as they are for evaluating print sources. But you should be alerted to some special problems on the Web. Some of the information that follows on Internet dangers and the organizations that help expose them is from an excellent book by Anne P. Mintz, ed. *Web of Deception: Misinformation on the Internet.* Medford: CyberAge Books, 2002.

Bias of Sponsors and Advertisers

Many sites that look very proper, perhaps even hosted by a prestigious organization contain biased data. For example, often medical research studies done by university staffs are sponsored by pharmaceutical companies. You should be aware that bias may exist in the reported results of such studies.

Bias of Special Interest Organizations

Thousands of organizations are interested in persuading you to take some action, promoting a political or social agenda, or seeking to change public policy. When you open the web site of an organization, be alert for biased information. The inexperienced researcher may accept a site's arguments as the only valid points of view on the subject. For example, the National Rifle Association and the Coalition to Stop Gun Violence hold very strong opposing views on the gun control issue.

Disinformation on Counterfeit Web Sites

Counterfeit web sites generate spurious information that the unsophisticated researcher believes is from a very reliable source. By using the real name of a site, but switching domain names from .gov to .org, for example, the perpetrators trick the researchers into believing they have found a legitimate site. Which of these sites is the correct one for President Obama? Try them both and see the results.

whitehouse.org whitehouse.gov

Many counterfeit sites are sponsored by racist, white supremacist, radical, or anti-government organizations with ideas well out of the mainstream of American thought. The martinlutherking.org site, for example, shown in Illustration 3.1. attempts to refute and denigrate the achievements of Dr. Martin Luther King. Still other counterfeit sites want to spoof regular sites.

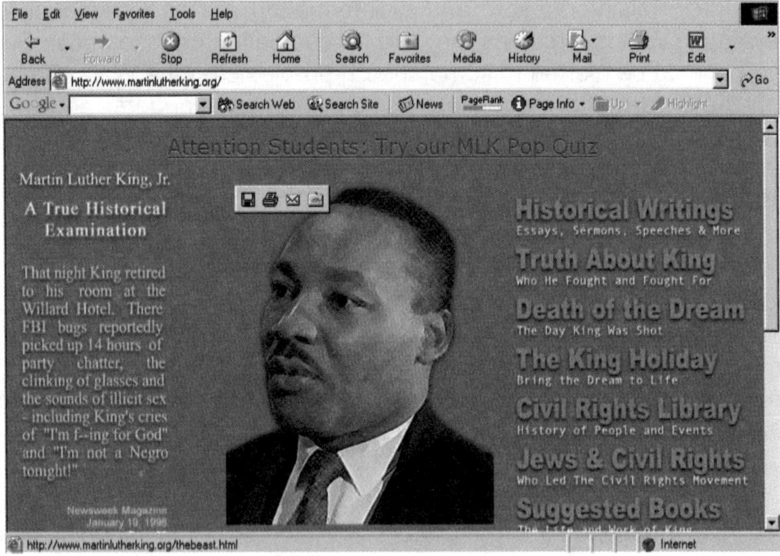

Illustration 3.1. Counterfeit Martin Luther King Web Site

Disinformation On Regular Web Sites

Disinformation, as you learned earlier, can be transmitted by governments eager to give their citizens and others incorrect information to control their thinking. This is especially true during wars and internal or international conflicts. For example, when American forces surrounded Baghdad during the Iraq war, the government of Sadam Hussein reported that U.S. troops were being overrun by loyalist soldiers when just the opposite was true. With conflicts arising in the Middle East, the Far East, and Europe, be alert for misinformation from various governernments.

Misinformation On Regular Web Sites

Misinformation, as defined earlier in this chapter, is incorrect information that is promulgated either intentionally or accidentally. For example, many Web sites purport to dispense medical and health information. However, many are loaded with misinformation. A search for a medical or health topic will yield sites advocating cures for cancer and hosts of other illnesses that are not supported by the medical establishment.

One of the most notorious misinformation sites is the Institute for Historical Review (http:ihr.org). It is one of several sites that deny that the Holocaust in Europe occurred during World War II. The site is replete with the names of several doctoral level scholars and claims complete objectivity. Despite the extensive historical record of the Holocaust, this organization continues to publish revisionist material.

Most will find the misinformation on such sites distasteful and anti-intellectual, but the First Amendment to our Constitution gives the revisionist historians and medical charlatans the freedom to publish what they will.

Problems With Newsgroups and Discussion Groups

A newsgroup is just like a bulletin board. Most are focussed on specific topics such as politics, health, economics. You can find newsgroups on just about any subject imaginable. There are some responsible, scholarly groups, but remember that anyone can post anything on a newsgroup site. Frequently, "conversations" take place among those who post messages. Unless the writer specifically identifies himself or herself you cannot know who the author is, nor can you be assured that the message is accurate.

Cautions About Weblogs or Blogs

Weblogs or blogs first appeared in the 1990s. Blogs are similar to personal websites, often updated, carrying "posts" in diary form. Blogs are rapidly replacing newsgroups. Anyone who owns a computer can become a blogger as several free web tools are available to those who wish to publish. Blog authors are free to express themselves, sometimes anonymously, on every conceivable issue and usually encourage readers to comment on their blog sites.

Blog posts can include text, images, sound, and video. Bloggers can quickly get news stories or comments out on the net. They frequently "scoop" regular TV news channels and newspapers.

Blogs exist for specific subjects such as medicine, law, politics, news, and literature and often include audio and video.

Blogs have rapidly grown in importance and influence. Major university schools of journalism have begun examining blogging and are comparing it to traditional journalism. Recently, blogs have catapulted into the nation's attention by breaking news in advance of traditional news sources or "correcting" mainstream media stories.

Here are three examples of the impact of blogs:

1. In 2002 Trent Lott, the Republican majority leader of the U. S. Senate, inadvertently praised Senator Strom Thurman for his racially segregationist views. Although the mainstream media failed to comment, bloggers quickly provided documents that eventually led to Lott's resignation as majority leader.

2. In 2006 Dan Rather of CBS News was contradicted by a blog that challenged his account of President Bush's military record resulting in his departure from the station.

3. Oprah Winfrey was attacked by bloggers about her touting of the putative non-fiction book by James Frey, *A Million Little Pieces,* that was later found to be faked, forcing her to make a public apology on TV.

When print or television journalists are reluctant to report stories that might embarrass advertisers or influential persons, bloggers can report without fear. Traditional journalists then feel free to report on the blogger's scoops. So weblogs can be very powerful communication tools.

Today blogs are used by major corporations, political parties, and politicians to get their messages out. Traditional media including television stations, newspapers, and magazines now publish their own blogs as do television and media personalities. Experts in various fields are blogging valuable and reliable information. Many blogs have taken on a mantle of respectability.

So what's the danger when using blogs? Simply, unless the blogger identifies him or herself, you cannot think about using the posting in your research. Even if the identity is known, you must carefully vet the posting to be sure you are not reading misinformation, disinformation, or a complete hoax. At best, you will usually be reading someone's opinion on a subject.

The researcher must identify only those blogs that meet the highest criteria and avoid those that do not or are suspect. Use all of the information listed above and in the Internet Source Evaluation Checklist that follows to be sure any blogs you use are worthwhile.

Concerns About Social Media: Facebook, LinkedIn, Twitter, MySpace, Digg, Reddit, Delicious, StumbleUpon, YouTube, Flickr, Etc.

These extremely popular social networking sites in Web 2.0 have mushroomed recently. People by the millions, and the number is increasing astronomically, subscribe to one or more of these sites to keep in touch with friends and co-workers and to share Internet sites and visuals. No doubt you are a subscriber.

The sites are becoming important sources of information. For example, governments, corporations, and other organizations have used YouTube video clips to get messages out quickly to counter bad publicity or to project a positive position. Occasionally, an alert person with a video camera will capture an incident that is newsworthy such as a speech by an important person not covered by traditional media. In 2009 a YouTube video of protests in Iran after the election of President Mahmoud Ahmadinejad may have been the first news of the conflict sent to the rest of the world.

Many newspapers, TV stations, businesses, organizations, and even the U.S. government have established Facebook, Twitter, and MySpace accounts through which they send and receive communications. Political parties have quickly recognized the power of the new Web 2.0 technology and are using text messaging and social networks to get out the vote and to build support for programs. Corporations respond quickly to modify a product or service because of the volume of negative "tweets" received.

Technology is rapidly being developed to help businesses and other organizations use Web 2.0. to gather and use information. Innovation in science and industry is now powered by ideas spread from the rank and file of corporations and organizations. This bottom-up movement is a radical change from the traditional top-down strategies traditionally used.

What does all this mean to you as a researcher? Be aware of the dangers of bias, hoaxes, misinformation, disinformation and personal chatter on Web 2.0. Many of the personal messages on Facebook, MySpace, and other social networks are unimportant. Individual tweets with gossip about what a friend is doing at the moment are not suitable for research.

However, some Web 2.0 material may be used as primary sources. See 3.2.1. Primary Print Sources. For example, you might use information in a politician's Facebook or a YouTube video of an incident shot by an amateur photographer to support a point in your paper. You will surely obtain lots of opinions.

Nevertheless, be sure to vet every Web 2.0 source. If you use an identifiable Facebook, MySpace or other social networking source, let your readers know why you think the information is important. For example, if you are researching global warming, you might find information on the Sierra Club Facebook page or that of ExxonMobil. You could appropriately use that material just as if it appeared on a regular Web site or in a print magazine. Facebook and other social networking sites have URLs to cite.

Illustration 3.2. shows the ExxonMobil Facebook page.

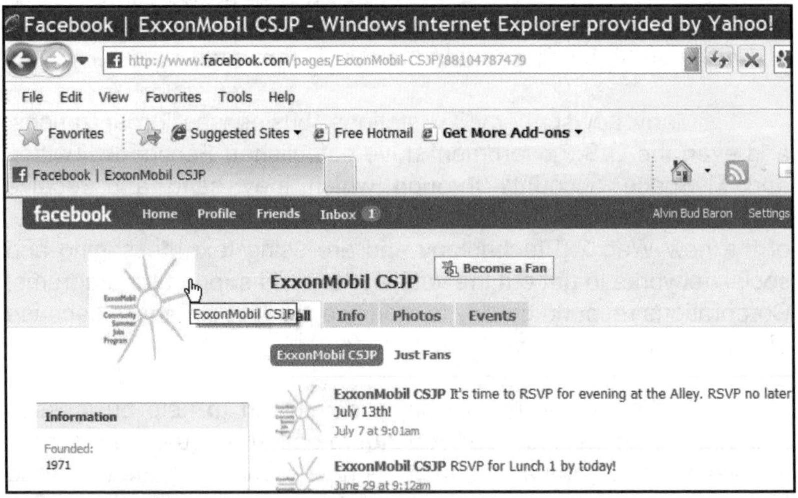

Illustration 3.2. ExxonMobil Facebook page.

Facebook pages always invite you to sign up for regular updates from the organization and become a Fan so you can receive regular updates on issues that interest you. Many organizations post Tweets that may lead you to further investigation.

You may be wondering how an organization's regular home page differs from a Facebook or other Web 2.0 page. Just below in Illustration 3.3. is the home page of ExxonMobil. This home page, like most others, contains the usual About and other tabs that will open pages to more information about the organization. Clicking on the energy & environment tab opens a page that describes how ExxonMobil plans to deal with greenhouse gas emissions. Facebook sites will usually contain more timely information and more links to other sites because they are continuously updated.

Illustration 3.3. ExxonMobil Home Page

The evolution of the Internet is continuing. By the time you read this chapter there may be several more social networking and communication sites and devices on the Internet. Just remember your responsiblity as a mature researcher. Maintain the highest standards of evaluation so you will never be discredited.

Internet Evaluation Checklist

- **Site:** Edu, org, gov, or mil sites maintained by colleges and universities, professional organizations, military, and governmental agencies are most reliable. Be cautious of .com sites that are usually filled with advertising and that may contain information for which payment has been made for publication. Be careful with blogs, newsgroups, and social networking sites. E-mail should be carefully evaluated and accepted only if it is a personal communication from a known expert.

- **Author:** Is the author well-known, expert, qualified? Is there an association with an established, recognized institution? If the author is an organization, check the About Us site.

- **Publisher:** Is the publisher a university, professional organization, government agency, or well-known publisher? Check web only publishers judiciously.

- **References:** Are quality sources cited which you can locate and check?

- **Currency:** Is information current with recent publication date? Look for the date the material was last updated.

- **Point of View:** Are facts rather than opinion presented? Is the author's point of view clear and supported by facts? Is the author's purpose to persuade, explain, or inform? Is the source a political activist or commercial lobby whose goal is to influence public opinion and legislation?

- **Audience:** Is information intended for mature, serious readers? Reject material that is frivolous or chatty.

- **Links:** Do hypertext links take you to educational or other solid sites which can lead to further reliable research and not to commercial sites?

- **Bibliography:** Is there a bibliography which attests to scholarship and leads to quality sources.

Task 4

Learn To Set Up Your Bibliography File

Task 4: Learn To Set Up Your Bibliography File

Suggested Time for Task 4: 1 Hour

4.1. Bibliography Files

Now that you have developed a Preliminary Thesis Question and understand how to evaluate sources, you are about to do some serious research in the physical library, on the Internet, and in databases. As you locate sources you must begin to keep a record of them in a Bibliography file. In this task you will learn how to set up your Bibliography file.

Your Bibliography file will form the basis of your MLA Works Cited list, your APA References list, your Turabian Bibliography or Reference list that you will insert at the end of your paper. Its purpose is to enable your reader to locate your sources, to explore the data more fully, and to check the accuracy of your research.

Print sources such as books typically are identified with standard bibliographic information such as the author's name, title, publisher, publication city and date of publication. Print journals add volume and issue numbers. Newspapers include editions. Magazines add dates of publication. Internet sources should be identified with similar bibliographic data that includes the name of the web site as well as the Internet URL address.

4.1.1. Decide On A Citation Style

Decide with your instructor which of the three citation styles you will use:

The Modern Language Association (MLA)

or

The American Psychological Association (APA)

or

Turabian - Based on the University of Chicago Style Manual

Each uses different styles for bibliography entries.

Microsoft Word and other software programs can create bibliography entries in all three citation styles. However, these programs are generally not helpful because they cannot generate all of the possible entries of all the styles. Therefore, it is probably easier to prepare your bibliography manually rather than to spend time editing the output of a word processor. The bibliography always appears at the end of your paper, but you must begin to compile the information as you find each source.

4.1.2. Posting Print Data

If your laptop or other portable electronic device is unavailable, you will have to photocopy any material you find in the library and note its bibliographic data or you can enter the data on 3 x 5 cards. When your computer is available, you can enter the information into your Bibliography file.

Here's how to post print data into your Bibliography file:

When you complete this exercise, you will know how to prepare your Bibliography file.

Open a new file and save it as Bibliography, Works Cited, or Reference depending on the citation style you are using.

Let's assume you are using the MLA style and your hypothetical Thesis Question is:

> How Does the Financial Crisis of 2008-9 Differ From the Great Depression of 1929-39?

You researched print material and located a book about the Great Depression by David Kennedy with the title, *Freedom From Fear* published in New York by Oxford University Press in 1999. You found information on pages 104-105 and you want to list it in your Works Cited file the way the MLA requires.

Your Works Cited file is open. Turn now to the MLA sample citations in Chapter 16. Look on page 16-5 and locate the correct MLA style for a book with one author. Did you find it? Good. Now scrupulously type the data for the Kennedy book matching the indention, underlining, periods, and commas of the sample.

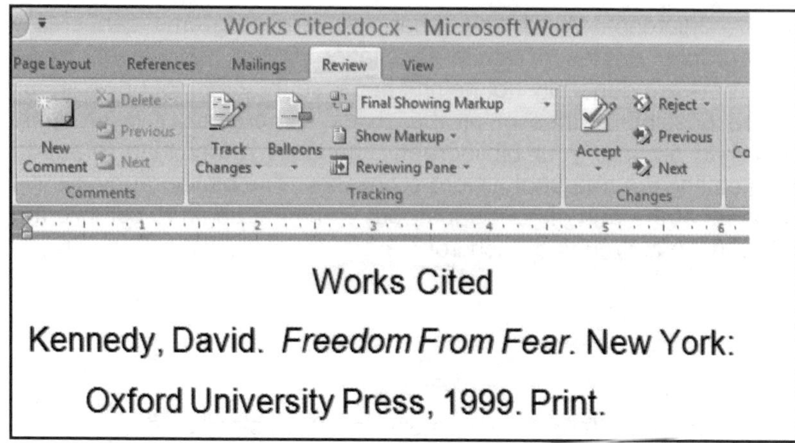

Illustration 4.1. Bibliography Entry For A One Author Book

Your entry should look exactly like Illustration 4.1. above.

As you continue your hypothetical research in the periodicals section of the library, you find an article by Peter Coy, titled "A Dogfight Over the Rescue Plan" on pages 018-019 in the March 30, 2009 issue of the magazine *BusinessWeek.*

Open your Works Cited file, move the cursor above the Kennedy entry to place the Coy article in correct alphabetical order by author's name. Off you go to page 16-11 to find the correct

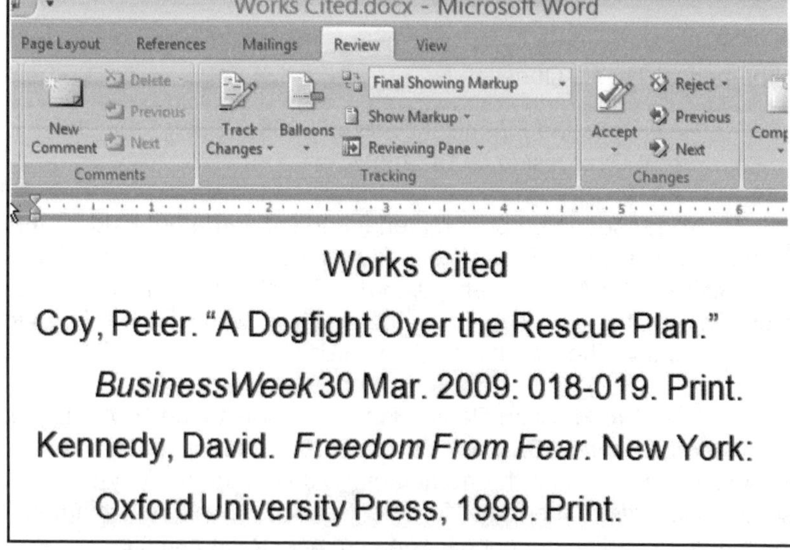

Illustration 4.2. Magazine Entry Added Above Book Entry

citation style for an article in a periodical magazine. Type the bibliographic information above the Kennedy entry. Compare your work with Illustration 4.2 on page 4-4 that shows the addition of the Coy entry.

4.1.3. Posting Internet Data

Citing Internet bibliographic data correctly is a bit trickier. Internet sites vary. Some print publications now offer Internet versions or separate online editions. Scholarly institutions, independent web sites, government organizations, businesses, libraries, and a host of bloggers populate the Web. Periodical articles, books, and a variety of written and audio-visual data are also available along with the many social networking sites like Twitter and Facebook.

Web sites often change or disappear and are frequently updated so the source you cite today may not be exactly the same at a later date. It is best to download or print sites you plan to use or move them to your favorites or bookmark files.

Web sites do not provide bibliographic data as clearly as print publications. For example, some online texts do not have page or paragraph numbers. It can be difficult to determine the various parts of a site. For example, is the name of the Web site the publisher or is there an underlying sponsor? Could the sponsor be the author? Try to be consistent and use the samples for Web sites in Chapters 16, 17, and 18 judiciously.

Here are some items you should try to identify in Web sites.

1. The name of any author, editor, translator, or other important contributor if given
2. The title of the book, journal, other work.
3. The title of the web site if the work is contained in one.
4. The edition or version.
5. The site's sponsor.or publisher.
6. The date of publication if given. Include the latest update.
7. The URL or Uniform Resource Locator or Internet address. Some URLs are so long and complicated that it is almost impossible to transcribe them accurately. Best method: Highlight the URL and copy-paste it into your Bibliography file. Divide

URLs only after double or single slashes. Never include your own punctuation.

8. The date you accessed the site.

Determining the various segments of an Internet site is difficult because one viewer may assume that the the overall domain name is the title of the site. Another viewer might think otherwise. Judgement comes into play here and there may be no really correct answer. Tip: Look at the URL. The major domain name is usually the publisher of the site.

Let's continue with this exercise. As you resume your hypothetical search for information on comparisons between the Great Depression and the 2008-9 financial crisis you Google the key words Unemployment Great Depression and get a promising site that is shown in Illustration 4.3. below.

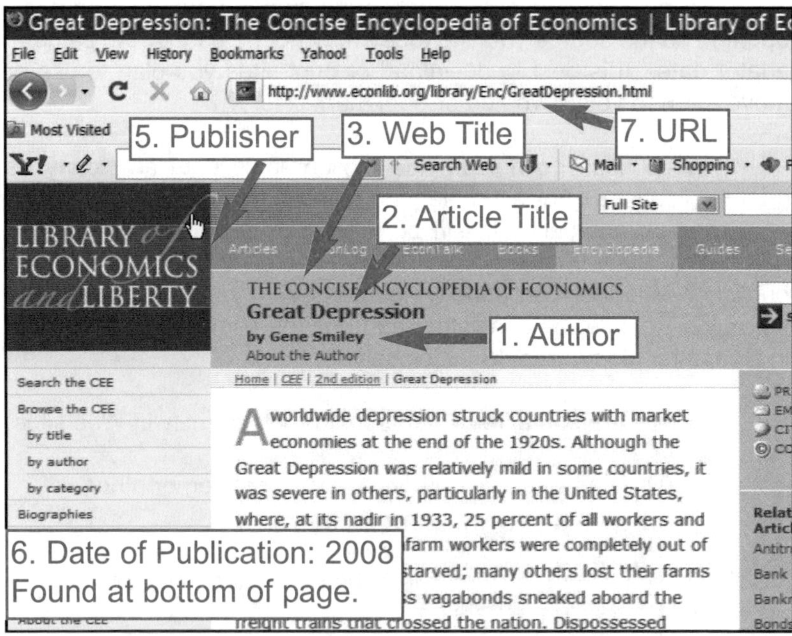

Illustration 4.3. Web Site On Great Depression

You carefully study the site looking for bibliographic data.

First: There is one author, Gene Smiley.

Second. The article title is "Great Depression."

Third: The Web site title is Concise Encylopedia of Economics

Fourth: There is no edition.
Fifth: The publisher is Library of Economics and Liberty.
Sixth: The date of publication is 2008.
Seventh: The URL is available.
Eighth: The date of access is May 25, 2009.

Turn now to Chapter 16 and locate the sample for a Nonperiodical Web publication. You should find it on pages 16-12 and 16-13. Carefully type the entry in alphabetical order. It should look like Illustration 4.4. below.

Remember, the purpose of the bibliography is to to enable your reader to find the same sources, to explore the data more fully, and to check the accuracy of your research. Here's a tip to be sure your reader can reach the same site.

Try to open the site using the information in your citation. If you easily get to your source, you have probably used an acceptable

Works Cited

Coy, Peter. "A Dogfight Over the Rescue Plan." *BusinessWeek* 30 Mar. 2009: 018-019. Print.

Kennedy, David. *Freedom From Fear.* New York: Oxford University Press, 1999. Print.

Smiley, Gene. "Great Depression." *Library of Economics and Liberty*, 2008. Web. 15 June 2009.

Illustration 4.4. Internet Entry Added To Bibliography

citation. For example, try reaching the site with the author's name and article title. If the site does not open, try using different entries until one opens the site. That entry should be included in your citation.

Your practice Bibliography file now contains three entries. You know how to locate samples for your sources in this book. You know how to keep track of your research findings in your Bibliography file. You understand the importance of maintaining a solid bibliography file of all the sources you consult, including those you may not use later. You have learned to use an important tool for researching.

Now that you have this skill under your belt, you can delete the practice entries you made. Of course, if you are using the APA Manual or Turabian, you should rename your Works Cited file as Reference or Bibliography as required.

You are now ready to move on to Task 5 in which you will learn how to set up your Note files.

Task 5

Learn To Set Up Your Note Files

Task 5: Learn To Set Up Your Note Files

Time for Task 5: 2 Hours

5.1. Note Taking

You have developed a Thesis Question, understand how to evaluate sources, and know how to build your Bibliography file. Now you must learn to use another important tool: In this task you will learn how to take notes from the sources you find and put them in your Note file.

Your quest is to find answers to your Thesis Question. You will locate information in print, on the Web, and in databases. As you read each source, you must decide how it relates to your Thesis Question. What points of view are expressed? Have you found opposing arguments? Does a source offer a good illustration or explanation of a point of view? Is a source an authority who can be quoted to support a position? Will statistical data in a source help answer your Thesis Question?

When you find good information, you must have a method of recording the data and keeping track of it so you can use it later to write your paper. You need a systematic, organized method of taking notes from the works you find. That's your Note file.

5.1.1. Quote, Summarize, or Paraphrase

There are three ways you can incorporate the material from sources into your paper.

Direct Quotation
Summary
Paraphrase

How are they different and how do you prepare them?

Quotations simply lift verbatim all the original writer's words and places them in your paper, word for word and enclosed in quotation marks. A quotation from a well-known authority is probably the most powerful technique for reinforcing a position. See the special instructions for placing quotations in your text in Chapters 16, 17, and 18 for the MLA, APA, and Turabian styles.

Paraphrases contain the author's ideas in your words. You should make no attempt to shorten the material. However, if you use any of the author's exact words, phrasing, or synonyms in any part of the paraphrase, you will be guilty of plagiarism. Because you are using the author's ideas without shortening, the paraphrase may be almost as effective as the quotation.

Summaries contain the author's ideas in your words, but in a shortened version. Just as with paraphrases, if you use any of the author's exact words, phrasing, or synonyms, you will be guilty of plagiarism.

5.2. Taking Notes From Print Sources

Follow all of the instructions for this exercise. You will prepare four practice Note files: a quotation, a summary, and a paraphrase from the same material as well as an Internet Note file.

Assume your Thesis Question is: How did William Wordsworth incorporate the major themes of the Romantic movement in his poetry? You find a book, *William Wordsworth,* by Russell Noyes published in New York by Twayne Publishers, Inc. On page 58 there is information about one of Wordsworth's poems, "Tintern Abbey," that looks promising. See Illustration 5.1. below.

Quote

Its repetitive words phrases, and patterns give to the flowing rhythms a wonderfully resonant and noble beauty. The poetic expression of the impact of the scenic landscape upon the innermost recesses of the poet's mind was as spontaneous as it was powerful. The poem took shape while his feelings were overflowing with excess of joy and while his faith in the power of nature to dispel "fear or pain or grief" was still at high tide. In after years he qualified and subdued his pronouncements in "Tintern Abbey' But he never lost delight in the simple converse of Nature or his faith that all created things can bring pleasure to the sensitive person impelled by love or praise.

Illustration 5.1 Original Noyes Material

Here's how to take notes from this source:

1. First, look at Illustration 5.2 on page 5-5 to see how the finished Note file will appear.
2. Open a New folder in My Documents and name it Notes.
3. Open a new page in Word and save it with the author's name, Noyes Note.
4. On the top line type the mimimum bibliographic data. You can find it on page 5-3 just above the Wordworth passage. You would already have prepared a Bibliography file, of course. Add the page number 58 and the call number.
5. Read the passage in Illustration 5.1. to learn what the material is about.
6. Copy the Subject tag from Illustration 5.2. Adding a Subject tag forces you to really think about how the content relates to your Thesis Question. You should use the same Subject tag for all notes from any source that relates to the same subject.
7. Copy the Comments line from Illustration 5.2. Comments are about any questions the piece raises, your reaction to it, or ideas about how you might use the information.
8. Read the passage and decide whether you will lift a direct quotation, summarize the passage, or paraphrase it.
9. For this exercise, you have decided to quote part of the material.

How To Quote

Look at the original passage in Illustration 5.1. The quotation that you want to place in your note file is in blue.

10. Type the word, Quotation, as a reminder.
11. Type the quote including punctuation, underlining, etc. Even errors should be copied and followed with the Latin word, [*sic*], "thus," in brackets and italicized. Enclose the passage in quotation marks. Change the font and color to differentiate the summary from your own writing. The quotation is in Book Antiqua. The other words are in Arial. When lifting a quotation carefully compare what you have copied and typed with the original to be sure it is an exact quotation.

12. Save the file and move it into your Notes folder in My Documents.
13. Compare your practice Noyes note file with Illustration 5.2. below. Did you get all the information correct? Do you understand the process?

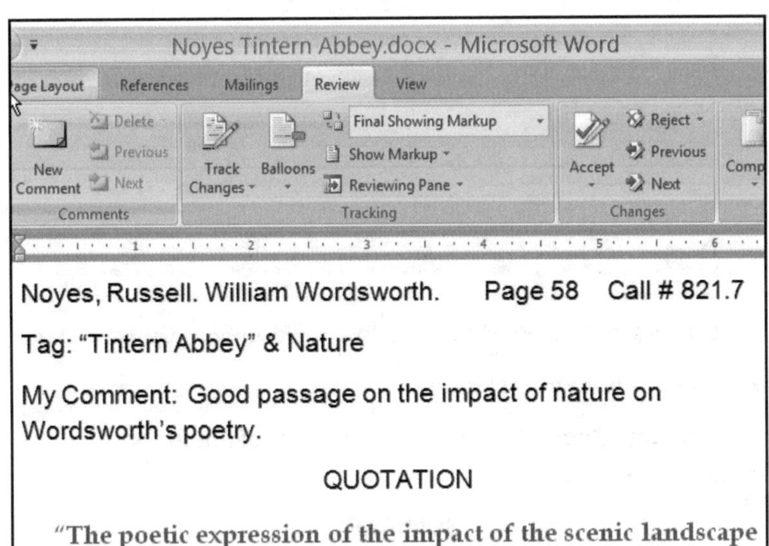

Noyes, Russell. William Wordsworth. Page 58 Call # 821.7

Tag: "Tintern Abbey" & Nature

My Comment: Good passage on the impact of nature on Wordsworth's poetry.

QUOTATION

"The poetic expression of the impact of the scenic landscape upon the innermost recesses of the poet's mind was as spontaneous as it was powerful."

Illustration 5.2. Sample Quotation Note File

How To Summarize

If you prepared a Note file identical to Ilustration 5.2, you know how to set up your Note files. But suppose you would rather summarize the entire piece instead of using a quotation. Here's how to do it:

Proceed through steps 1 - 7 on page 5-4. Type the word, Summary. Read the original passage. Do not look at it again. Try to summarize the author's words in your own but do not include any of your own ideas or interpretations. Don't peek at Illustration 5.3. You may not use any of the author's own words, synonyms,or phrasing or you will be guilty of plagiarism. Type your summary in your Note file. Change the font and color to differentiate the summary from your own writing. Be sure the summary is shorter than the original.

Read the original again and compare it with your summary to check for accuracy. Make necessary revisions and corrections. Now check your work against that in Illustration 5.3 below. How does your summary compare with the illustration. Note that none of the author's words or phrasing is used. Summarizing requires some new skills, so practice with other paragraphs in your history or English texts.

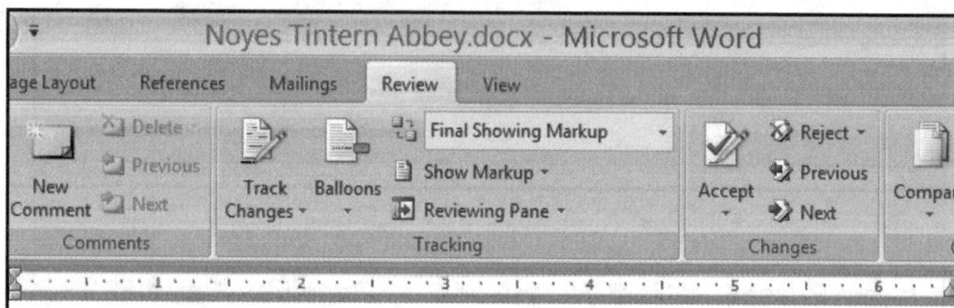

Noyes, Russell. William Wordsworth. Page 58 Call # 821.7

Tag: "Tintern Abbey" & Nature

My Comment: Good passage on the impact of nature on Wordsworth's poetry.

SUMMARY

The rhythm and phrasing of "Tintern Abbey reflect the strong feeling developed in Wordsworth as he reacted to Nature's landscapes. Later his belief in the power of nature was less fervent, although he always loved the simple joys it brought.

Illustration 5.3. Sample Summary Note File

How To Paraphrase

Let's assume you decide to paraphrase the material. Here's how to do it:

Proceed through steps 1 - 7 on page 5-4. Type the word, Paraphrase. Read the original passage. Do not look at it again. Try to paraphrase the author's words in your own but do not include any of your own ideas or interpretations. Don't peek at Illustration 5.4. You may not use any of the author's own words, synonyms, or phrasing or you will be guilty of plagiarism.

Type your paraphrase in the Note file. Read the original again and compare it with your paraphrase to check for accuracy. Make necessary revisions and corrections. Compare your work with that in Illustration 5.4. below. How does your paraphrase compare with the illustration. Note that none of the author's words or phrasing are used. Change the font and color to differentiate the summary from your own writing. Paraphrasing, like summarizing, is not easy. and requires some practice. Try paraphrasing a few passages in your history, science, or English texts to help you get the hang of it.

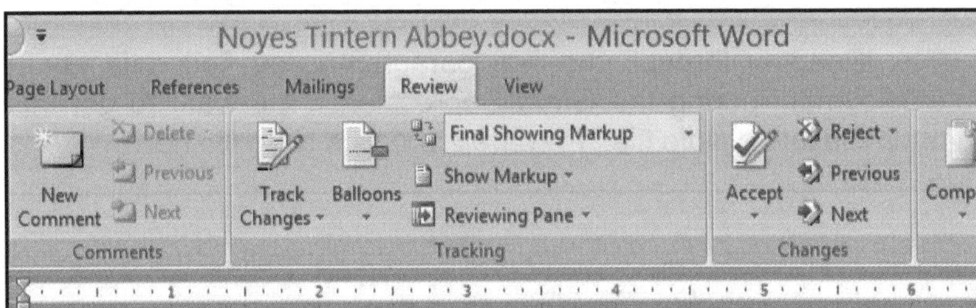

Noyes, Russell. William Wordsworth. Page 58 Call # 821.7

Tag: "Tintern Abbey" & Nature

My Comment: Good passage on the impact of nature on Wordsworth's poetry.

PARAPHRASE

"Tintern Abbey" reflects the powerful emotions of near ecstasy Wordsworth felt at the time. The poem's content and form are an outgrowth of the effect of the natural landscape on the poet and his belief that nature could shield mankind from the sadness and pain of life. As he grew older he was less enthusiastic about the ability of nature to soothe the troubled spirit. Nevertheless, he continued to derive joy from communing with nature.

Illustration 5.4. Sample Paraphrase Note File

5.3. Taking Notes From Internet Sources

Getting notes into your Note file from the Internet is easier than taking notes from print materials. You can search the Internet, locate sources, and take notes anywhere you have access to a computer or even a mobile device such as an iphone, Palm, or Blackberry.

Remember In Task 4 there was a search for information comparing the Great Depression with the 2008-2009 economic crisis? The search key words in Google were Unemployment Great Depression. The site found is shown again in Illustration 5.5. on the next page.

Reading through the first paragraph, you find data about unemployment during the Great Depression. You want to get this information into a Note file. Prepare a practice Note file now. Here's how to do it:

1. Open a new Note file and save it as Smiley, the author of the Internet site.
2. Enter the minimum bibliographical data necessary to tie it to its Bibliography file. You can copy-paste the URL and any other significant bibliographic data from the Internet site directly to the Note file. If pages or paragraphs are numbered on the site, be sure to include them in the Note file.
3. Minimize the Internet site.
4. Add a Subject tag to identify the nature of the content. A good tag for this note might be **Unemployment - Great Depression.**
5. Add your Comments about how you might use the data, any questions the piece raises, or your reaction to it. For example, you might write: **Unemployment not so high in 2008-2009. Why so high in Great Depression?**
6. Read the passage, locate the material you want to use. It's circled in blue. Decide whether you will quote, summarize the passage, or paraphrase it.
7. You are going to quote, so copy-paste the quotation directly into your Note file.
8. Change the font and color to differentiate the summary, quote, or paraphrase from your own writing to avoid plagiarism.
9. Save the file. Move it into the My Documents Note Folder.

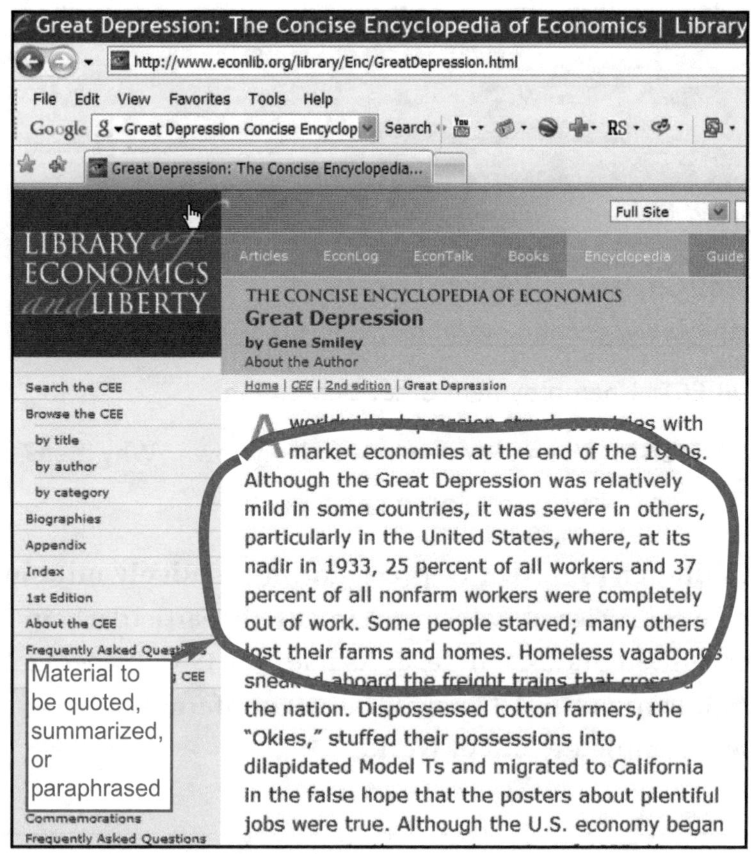

Illustration 5.5. Internet Site

Compare your practice Internet Note file with Illustration 5.6 on page 5-10. Your practice file and the illustration should be identical.

Through this exercise you have prepared four Note files and learned how to add quotations, summaries, and paraphrases from your sources. You can produce great Note files from print and Internet sources.

If you find other material in the site that could be used in another part of your paper, just open another Note file and save it as Smiley - with a different subject. For example, you might be writing about bank failures in the Depression. Open a new file and save it as Smiley - Bank Failures and follow the procedures above. You might have Note files named, Noyes-Romantic Themes and Noyes-"Daffodils." Of course, you can do the same with print sources.

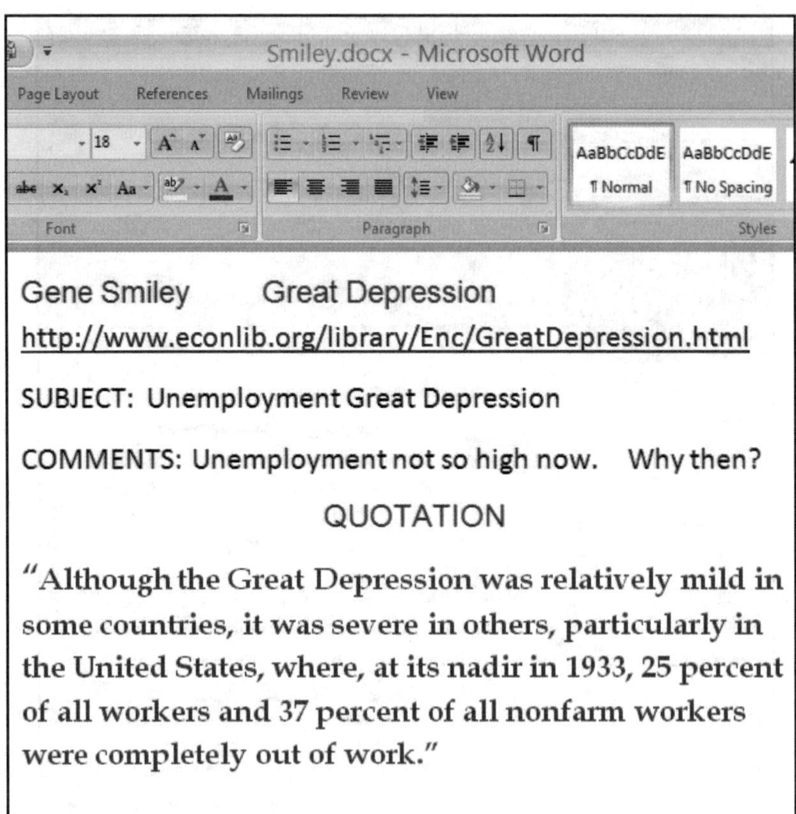

Illustration 5.6. Sample Internet Note File

5.4. Delaying The Insertion of Quotations, Summaries or Paraphrases

At early stages in your research you may want to wait until you have a clearer idea about how to develop your thesis before deciding how to use your sources. If so, just photocopy the page or pages of print material or paste whole passages from the Internet into a Note file with the name of the author and subject.

5.5. No Computer Available in the Library?

If you have no computer available when you are searching in the library, take your notes on 5 x 8 file cards. When your computer is available, transfer the information into your Note files.

Task 6

Search The Physical Library

Task 6: Search The Physical Library

Time for Task 6: 5-6 Hours

You now have the tools you need to be a competent research writer. You selected a topic and developed a Thesis Question. You learned to evaluate print and Internet sources. You know how to set up your Bibliography and Note files. You are ready to begin your search for information about your Thesis Question with intensive research.

6.1. Six Goals of Research

First, to get an overview of the subject you have chosen.
Second, to determine if there is enough high quality information quality available.
Third, to evaluate sources for recency, author's reputation, scholarship, relevance, and objectivity.
Fourth, to begin accumulating source material.
Fifth, to develop your own point of view on the subject.
Sixth, to formulate a Thesis Statement from your Thesis Question.

By conducting research you will learn how other authors have dealt with the topic of your Thesis Question. You will find writers who have explored different aspects of the subject. Some will be in agreement and others will hold opposing views. You may discover new viewpoints that had not occurred to you.

As you study each source, you should gradually develop your own point of view. Ask yourself, "What do I think about this question?" "What will I try to prove to my readers?" Eventually, you will have a clearer idea of how you want to approach your subject. Become enthusiastic and passionate about your beliefs. The most important part of selecting a Thesis Question is to make a personal investment in it. Don't be surprised if you find that your ideas and focus begin to change as you read and digest different sources.

You will need at least five and possibly more sources depending on the scope of your assignment. Your sources may include books, articles in journals and magazines, and information from reference books and Internet sites. If you do not find a number of suitable sources you may have to return to Task 2 to find a topic that has more information available.

Remember, you must evaluate each source to determine whether it meets the tests of recency, author's reputation, scholarship, relevance, objectivity, and accuracy.

Just as you needed an organized note taking system, you also need to approach your research in an orderly manner beginning in the physical library. With the Internet so easily available and since Google has become a verb, many students overlook the valuable resources in their school and community libraries.

6.2. Physical Library Organization

The library is the place to start. It is better than the Internet in the initial search because you can zero in on the best print reference works in your field rather than get the thousands of sites that pop up when you enter terms in a search engine.

Your school library has undoubtedly conducted orientation lectures about the various collections.and how they can be accessed. You may have found them boring in the past, but now is the time to ask the library media specialist for help.

Don't be shy. Let the librarian know what you are looking for in the terms of your Thesis Question. Say something like, "I am trying to find out why the unemployment rates during the Great Depression were so much higher than the rates during the 2008-2009 financial crisis." You will certainly be sent in the right direction.

Let's review how your library is organized so you will be familiar with all that it has to offer. Library collections of materials are usually arranged as follows:

6.2.1. Bound Print Book Collection

The collection of bound print books is kept on shelves called stacks. These books are assigned "call numbers" based on the Dewey Decimal System or the Library of Congress System. Become familiar with these two systems and you will feel more confident.

The Dewey Decimal Classification is used by most public libraries and school libraries. The system is divided into ten main classes as shown below. Each main class is further divided into ten divisions, and each division into ten sections. The first digit in each three-digit number represents the main class. For example, 500 represents natural sciences and mathematics and is used for general works in the sciences.

The second digit in each three digit number indicates the division. For example, 510 is used for mathematics, 520 for astronomy, and 530 for physics. The third digit in each three digit number indicates the section. Thus, 530 is used for general works on physics, 531 for classical mechanics, and 532 for fluid mechanics.

A decimal point follows the third digit in a class number after which division by ten continues to the specific degree of classification needed. For example, the title, *Freedom From Fear: the American People in Depression and War, 1929-1945* by David Kennedy, is classified as 973.91 K indicating all the divisions and sub-divisions under the 970 heading, General History of North America. The letter K designates the first letter of the author's last name.

Dewey Decimal Classification System	
000	Generalities
100	Philosophy and Psychology
200	Religion
300	Social Sciences
400	Language
500	Natural Sciences and Mathematics
600	Technology (Applied Sciences)
700	The Arts
800	Literature and Rhetoric
900	Geography and History

The Library of Congress system uses a series of letters rather than numerals for the major divisions as shown below. All entries can begin with one, two, or three letters. The first letter of a call number represents one of the 21 major divisions of the LC system. For most of the subject areas, the first letter represents books of a general nature for that subject area. For example, Q stands for Science.

The title, *Freedom From Fear: The American People in Depression and War, 1929-1945* by David Kennedy, has the call number E173.094.

That call number contains all the letters and numerals that identify the divisions and sub-divisions of the Library of Congress system. The letter E in the example above tells you that the subject is American history. The numeral 173 indicates that the book deals with Sources and Documents while the numeral .094 describes further classification.

Library of Congress Classification System	
A General Works	P Language and Literature
B Philosophy, Psychology, Religion	Q Science
C History - Auxiliary Sciences	R Medicine
D History - American	S Agriculture
E & F History: American	T Technology
F Geography, Anthropology	U Military Science
H Social Sciences	V Naval Science
J Political Science	Z Bibliography and Library Science
K Law	
L Education	I,O,W,X, and Y are not being used. They are available for future expansion and for classifying knowledge yet to be discovered.
M Music	
N Fine Arts	

Ask your media specialist how to access the collections.and explain anything that you do not understand.

6.2.2. The Reference Section

The reference section houses most of the print reference materials such as encyclopedias, yearbooks, atlases, indexes, dictionaries, and other specialized reference books. There are good reasons to visit your library's Reference Section before hitting the Internet.

First, you will meet a professional library media specialist. He or she is trained in research techniques and will be happy to help you with your search.

Second, you will familiarize yourself with the standard print reference works and reference tools. Every field has specialized reference books such as encyclopedias, indexes, bibliographies, research guides, biographical indexes, dictionaries, and statistical summaries.

Prepare to Photocopy Bibliography and Note Files

If your laptop or other portable electronic device is unavailable, you will have to photocopy any note material you find in the library and copy its bibliographic data. When your computer is available, you can enter the data into your Bibliography and Note files. See 6.5. and 6.6. on page 6-14.

SEARCH ENCYCLOPEDIAS

In addition to the general encyclopedias, you will find special encyclopedias on virtually every subject.

General Encyclopedias

Encyclopedia Americana
Encyclopedia Britannica

Some Special Encyclopedias

Encyclopedia of Asian History
Encyclopedia of Biological Sciences
Encyclopedia of Psychology
Encyclopedia of Social Work
Encyclopedia of World Art

SEARCH BIBLIOGRAPHIES

Bibliographies contain lists of publications arranged by subject. There are bibliographies of bibliographies, bibliographies of general subjects, and bibliographies of special fields. There are even bibliographies of reference books - a good place to start.

The general bibliographies listed below will lead you to lists of titles on your subject. The special bibliographies should help too.

Popular General Bibliographies

Bibliographic Index: A Cumulative Bibliography of Bibliographies
The New York Times Guide To Reference Materials
Subject Guide to Books In Print

Some Special Bibliographies

American Women and Politics
Bibliographic Guide to Black Studies
Bibliographic Guide to Business and Economics
MLA Bibliography
Political Science: A Bibliographic Guide to the Literature

SEARCH ABSTRACTS

An abstract is a summary of an article. Almost every discipline publishes volumes that summarize articles from the journals in the field. If you find an abstract that looks valuable, get the journal and read the full text. If the journal is not in the library, it is permissible to cite information from an abstract as long as you use the appropriate citation. You may also find the full text of an article on the Internet.

Special Subject Abstracts

Art Abstracts
Biological Abstracts
Cambridge Scientific Abstracts
General Science Abstracts
Criminal Justice Abstracts
Dissertation Abstracts
ERIC - Education Abstracts
Historical Abstracts
Humanities Abstracts
Newspaper Abstracts
Periodical Abstracts
Psychological Abstracts
Social Sciences Abstracts
Sociological Abstracts

SEARCH DICTIONARIES

Dictionaries contain alphabetically arranged brief definitions of terms within specific disciplines. They are excellent for obtaining precise meanings of unfamiliar terms in your area of research.

Popular Dictionaries

American Dictionary of Economics
Black's Law Dictionary
Dictionary of Biology
Dictionary of Botany
Dictionary of Music
Dictionary of Philosophy
Dictionary of the Social Sciences

SEARCH BIOGRAPHICAL SOURCES

Volumes of biographical data are published for persons living and dead. In addition, some disciplines publish biographical data on prominent persons in specific fields. If your research deals with a person, these sources will provide brief biographical summaries which can serve as a starting point before going on to full biographies.

Biographical Sources For Living Persons

Biography Index   Current Biography
Who's Who in America
International Who's Who

Biographical Sources For Deceased Persons

American National Biography
Webster's New Biographical Dictionary

Biographical Sources In Specific Disciplines

Who's Who in Religion
American Men and Women of Science
Biographical Dictionary of Women Artists in Europe and America Since 1850
Dictionary of American Negro Biography
Dictionary of Literary Biography

SEARCH RESEARCH GUIDES

Research guides contain reference tools and other sources available for research in a particular discipline. Ask your librarian for the latest research guides in the area of your Thesis Question.

Research Guides

Library Research Guide to History
Literary Research Guide

SEARCH YEARBOOKS

Yearbooks contain information about specific personalities, discoveries, inventions, or other events which occurred during a specific year. To locate such current information use one of the following.

Typical Yearbooks

Americana Annual
Britannica Book of the Year

SEARCH STATISTICAL SOURCES

Statistical data is available from many sources, particularly government agencies. If your research deals with such data, ask your librarian for help finding specialized statistical information.

Statistical Data Publications

Demographic Yearbook
Statistical Abstract of the United States
Statistical Yearbook

SEARCH INDEXES

General indexes catalog articles from popular newspapers and magazines. Specialized indexes catalog articles from journals within a discrete discipline. They are published periodically and are usually bound in volumes containing a range of dates. Ask your librarian for help in finding the print specialized indexes.

General Indexes

New York Times Index
Reader's Guide to Periodical Literature

Special Indexes

American Humanities Index
American Women's History Index
Ancient History and Culture
Art Index
Biology Digest
Book Review Digest
Education Index
General Science Index
Literary Criticism Index
Sociological Index

6.2.3. The Periodical Section

All the magazines and journals the library subscribes to are housed in the periodicals section. Current editions of magazines and some scholarly journals are usually arranged on open shelves in alphabetical order, but back issues generally are bound periodically and are obtained at the reference desk.

The best way to search for your subject in periodicals is to use the *Reader's Guide to Periodical Literature*. The *Guide* lists every article in a large number of magazines by subject and author. It is published monthly, with quarterly and annual summaries.

One alphabetized list contains all the entries for authors and subjects. Reviews of movies, books, radio and television are listed under the subject such as Motion Picture Reviews or Theatre Reviews. Fiction works are listed by author under the heading Fiction - Single Works. Look through the first pages of the Guide for more information on its arrangement of entries.

As you search the Reader's Guide and find suitable articles for your Thesis Question, jot down the magazine or journal titles. Then go to the media specialist for the list of your library's magazine and journal subscriptions. You may be disappointed to learn that the article you think is perfect is in a journal your library does not own.

6.2.4. Special Collections Section

Many libraries have special collections of various types. For example, some libraries are depositories of old local newspapers and documents. Rare historical documents such as deeds and maps are frequently available to researchers. These items deteriorate with age and are often available in microfiche, microform, and microfilm and are readable with special viewing machines.

Special collections may be housed in separate areas. For example, the New York Public Library has a map room where current and old maps are kept. Virtually all libraries now house audio and video tapes, CDs, DVDs and other recorded material in a special collections area. Be sure to ask your library media specialist about the special collections available. You may be surprised to find there is a trove of information on your Thesis Question.

6.2.5. The Online Catalog

Most university and municipal libraries and many secondary schools have online catalogs. There are many different online catalog programs so the specifics of searching will vary, but they all basically follow similar procedures.

You can probably access your school's online catalog from home or from your dorm with your own computer or from terminals in the library or other places around campus. In addition to the resources of your own school library, you may find links to:

1. Other district school's library sites.
2. The local public library's online site.
3. Your state or county library system site.
4. Commercial databases.

If you can access your county or state system, you will find links to more extensive holdings. You will need your library card number or other password and user name to gain access to remote library sites.

You can search the online catalog in several ways:

1. Author - If you enter an author's name, a list of all of the works by that author held in the library's collection will appear on the screen.

2. Title - If you enter the title, the screen will display the works with that title.
3. Subject - If you enter a major subject heading similar to the subject headings in the Dewey Decimal System or Library of Congress systems such as *American Presidents,* the screen will display all the works held under that heading.
4. Keyword - Keyword searches will produce lists of works that contain the keyword in a work's title or subject heading, such as *Andrew Jackson and Cherokee Indians.*

Illustration 6.1 is a typical online catalog search box. Assume you are looking for a book by David Kennedy and are not quite sure of the title so you type his name and click on the author button.

Illustration 6.1 Typical Online Catalog Search Box

All of the books held in the library by David Kennedy appear on the next screen. The fourth title in the list is Freedom From Fear, the book you are seeking, as shown in Illustration 6.2. below.

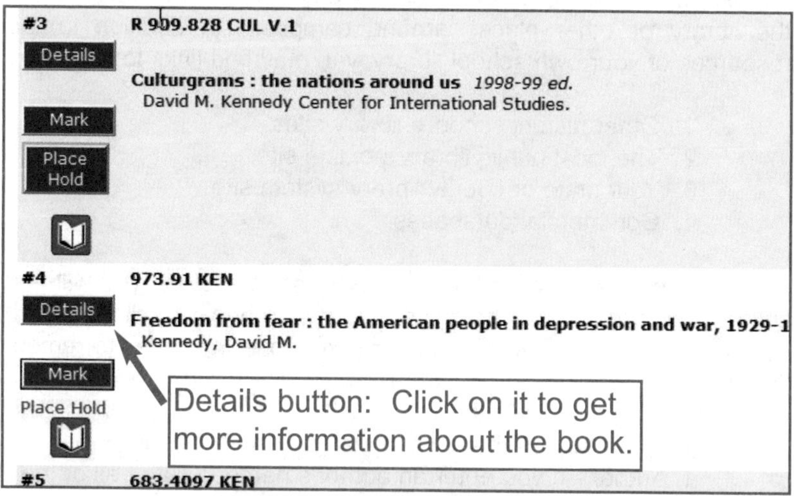

Illustration 6.2. Typical Listing of Books By An Author

But in this system there is limited information beyond the call number. You click on the Details button and a screen similar to the one shown in Illustration 6.3 appears.

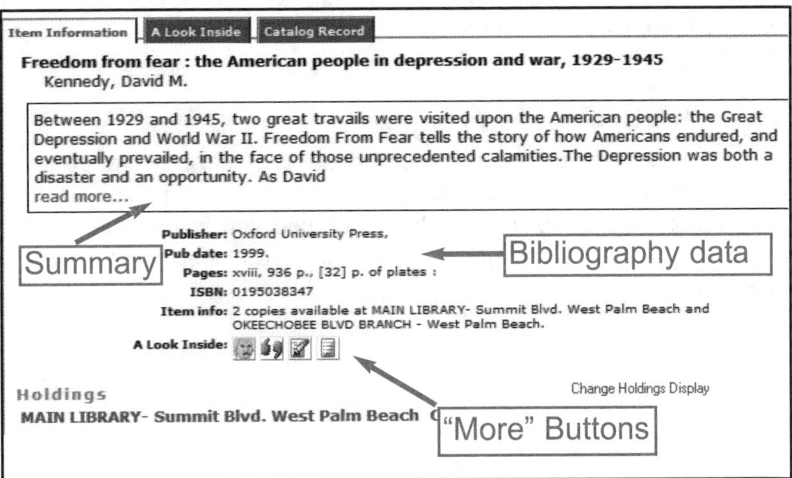

Illustration 6.3. Typical Full Bibliographic Online Entry

Details screens provide all of the bibliographic information you need for your Bibliography file plus the library call number plus a synopsis of the book. Frequently there will be a picture of the book jacket. Other buttons may provide a summary of the book, the table of contents, a book review, or the author's biography.

Some details screens have a More On This Topic button that will generate a list of all the library's holdings on the subject. If you were working on the Great Depression, you would be given a list of 8 or 9 other books including the works of Arthur Schlesinger, a famous 20th century historian. Some screens will give you a list of books that are physically near the Kennedy book on the shelves in the library.

Other details screens offer a More On This Author button that will generate books that have information about or by David Kennedy.

The online catalog is a very powerful tool that can energize your search by giving you much information on your Thesis Question. Very quickly you can find many related sources. Using the online catalog is like having a personal librarian!

6.5. Prepare Bibliography Files

As you find suitable sources, enter each in alphabetical order in your Bibliography file. Check Chapters 16, 17, or 18 for the correct citation format for the style you are using. Look back at Task 4 if you need to review how to do this.

6.6. Prepare Note Files

After entering each source in your Bibliography file, prepare a Note file for each. Be sure you include minimum bibliography information at the top of each file to enable you to find the source again if needed. Look back at Task 5 if you need to review the procedure.

Task 7

Search The Internet

Task 7: Search The Internet

Time for Task 7: 5 Hours

Now that you have met the reference media specialist and completed your search in the physical library you can move on to the Internet search.

In Task 3.3.1. The Internet in Perspective, you learned how the Internet has changed the way information is produced and disseminated. You understand how carefully you must evaluate all material you find on the Web. Although you may think that Internet searching is faster and easier than a library search, be aware of the possible pitfalls.

7.1. Conducting Internet Research

Just as you conducted careful research in the physical library, you must be purposely methodical and organized when searching the Internet.

Think of all the times you have Googled to get a "quick and dirty" overview of a subject. A friend tells you about a hot, new band so you jump to the Internet and Google the name. In an instant you get pages of sites about the latest musical sensation.

However, serious Internet searching is not quite so simple. According to Microsoft researchers, most Google searchers find what they are looking for only 50 percent of the time and some are just plain frustrated. When you enter terms in the search box, Google's results pages list the titles of thousands of journal articles, digitized books, blogs, graphics, video, and sound. The sites are sponsored by publishers, organizations, government agencies and businesses as well as bloggers and social networkers. Unfortunately, the Internet is like a vast library that has no regular plan of cataloging such as the Dewey Decimal or the Library of Congress systems. It is best to review some Internet protocols before you begin.

7.1.1. Uniform Resource Locators - URLs

Internet addresses are similar to regular mail addresses in function, but are more complicated. The URL contains a series of network names separated by dots (.), slashes (/), and tildes (~).

URLs are very specific. Some are case sensitive, which means if some of the letters are capitalized, you must be sure those are capitalized when typing the address. An extra space, period, or other miscue will make it impossible to reach the site.

7.1.2. Internet Address Domains:

The last part of a URL is its domain name. Listed below are the most common domain names in current use.

.com........commercial and business
.edu.........educational institutions
.gov.........government agencies
.mil..........military organizations
.net..........network resources
.org..........other organizations

For example, http://starburst.uscolo.edu means there is a sub-network called starburst connected to a network at the University of Southern Colorado and it is an educational institution. The address, http://www.ed.gov is the U.S. Department of Education Online Library. A two letter country abbreviation usually ends the address when a country is designated.

You can be most confident researching .edu, .gov, and .mil domain sites. The .org sites are sponsored by organizations that may have biased agendas, but don't rule them out entirely. Bona fide organizations such as historical societies, museums, and educational foundations frequently use .org domains. The .coms are business sites so also use caution. Checking the domain name first may save you from going down the wrong path.

7.2. Google Search Engine Search

Although there are several popular search engines, the best three are Google, Yahoo, and Bing. However, you have to help the engine do its job effectively. Because of the vast number of documents available on the Internet, a simple one word query to a search engine will produce many thousands of sites. Skilled researchers know how to use the best search key word terms to optimize their searches.

When results pages appear, Internet searchers are often frustrated and confused looking for relevant Web sites. Sometimes search engines list the most often visited site first. Although the site may be seen by many searchers, it may not have any useful research information. Businesses pay search engines to list their products at the top of results pages. These sites crowd the pages adding to the confusion.

Search engines do not think like human beings. When you enter a key word such as *Obama* in the search box, the engine "looks" at millions of Web sites and will show those that contain your key word without regard to the context. Google will not understand that you really want to know how Obama chooses Supreme Court justice nominees. If you want that information, you will have to give Google better directions in the form of precise key words. In addition, all search engines use "operators" to help you use your key words. See 7.2.3. to see how to refine your key words.

The success of your search depends on two factors:

- your choice of the best key words
- your skill in using the engine's special "operators."

You must understand the "operators" that Google uses to optimize your search and you must be very specific with key words.

7.2.1. Google "Operators"

Listed below are some Google operators Other engines use similar operators.

Phrase search - If you want Google to find words exactly in order, enclose the words in double quotation marks as in "Unemployment In Great Depression." However, Google will probably miss many sites that contain those words but not in the order within the quotation marks. In most cases the phrase search is not necessary because Google recognizes words in order and will usually find all the words.

OR - If you want Google to find files containing at least one of the words, insert a capital OR between them. For example, if you enter President Obama OR Vice President Biden, only files containing at least one of the terms will appear.

intitle - If you want to find all the sites that contain some specific words in the titles, type the word, intitle, followed by a colon and the specific words you seek in the titles like this:

intitle:Great Depression.

site: - If you want to search for information in a particular Web site or domain, enter the key word followed by a colon and add the domain or Web site. For example, if you want to get data only from the .gov domain, type Great Depression:.gov. Or you might enter Great Depression:New York Times to find all the sites only in the New York Times Web site.

7.2.2. Google Advanced Searching

Google simplifies some of its operators by placing them in a template in its Advanced Searching screen. By entering your key words in the appropriate blanks you will define your search to make it easier for the engine to find what you want. You reach Advanced Search by clicking on the Advanced Search link to the right of the regular search box.

7.2.3. Refine Google Key Words

Even more important than using "operators" is your choice of key words. Choosing the wrong key words will result in frustration. Try to use as few terms as possible. Keep it simple. Here's how to do it:

Step 1. Examine your Thesis Question and identify the key words that are most likely to produce the best results. Try to be as specific as possible.

Thesis Question: How have U. S. businesses reacted to global warming?

Possible Key Words:

global warming U. S. business

Step 2. List the possible combinations that may narrow the search using the appropriate "operators."

Possible Improved Key Words and Phrases:

global warming "power plants"
global warming "auto industry"
global warming economy
global warming business

You do not need the phrase operator quotation marks around the words, global warming, but you might need them around power plants and auto industry. If not successful, keep trying new combinations of key words and operators.

7.2.4. Trouble Shooting Search Problems

Unrelated documents in results?

Use correct spelling of all key words.

Too many documents or unrelated documents?

Use phrase searching.
Use advanced search procedures.

Too few documents?

Use OR to broaden search.
Use less specific and fewer key words.
Click on Related Articles link under site title.

Last resort:

Look for hints on the engine's results page or Help link.

7.2.5. Typical Google Search

Let's assume you were interested in the Thesis Question: How did slavery affect political parties in New York State? You entered the key words Draft Riots of 1863 Democratic Party. Illustration 7.1 on the next page shows a part of the results page that Google provides.

As you can see, Google found about 26,100 sites that contained the key words. Google arranges the results with the most relevant and most recent first. This illustration shows only the top three, but the page contains about nine more sites.

7.2.6. Analyze the Results Page

Study each result on the page in this example carefully to determine if it will be valuable. Each entry contains several elements:

First line: The Web site title underlined. An underlined term is a link. The New York City Draft Riots of 1863.

Second line: A brief synopsis of the site's content.
Democratic leaders raised the specter of a New York deluged with...in July 1863, white longshoremen took advantage of the chaos of the Draft Riots...

Third line: The URL of the site with its size is on the third line.
http://www.press.uchicago.edu/Misc/Chicago/317749.html - 29k

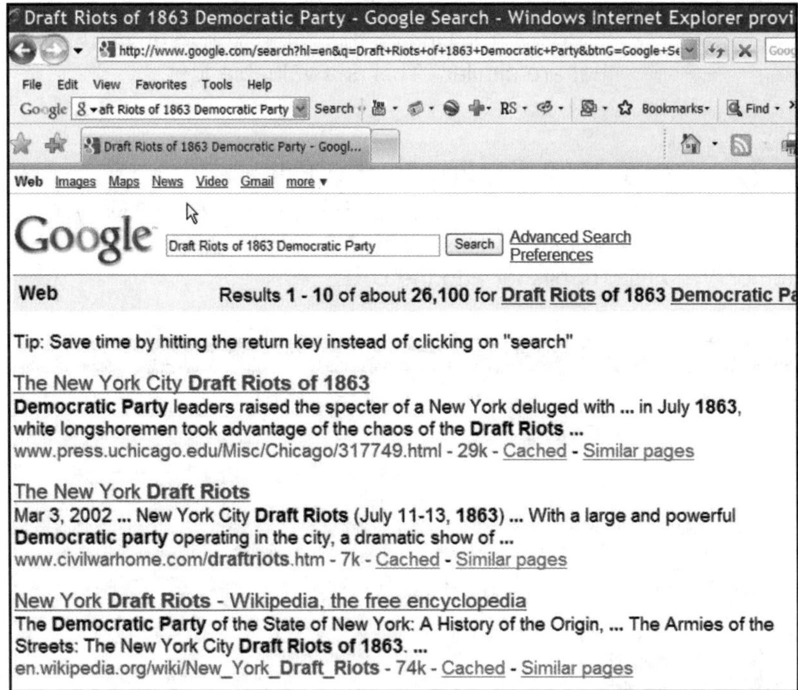

Illustration 7.1. Typical Google Results Page

Look at the URL under each entry to find the .edu and .gov domains first. Then look for .org's of appropriate organizations with good credentials.

"The New York City Draft Riots of 1863," looks promising because its URL is a .edu from the University of Chicago.

Third line: The word, Cached, follows the URL on the third line. This term indicates that Google has taken a snapshot of the page and has placed it in a back-up file in case it is not available on the day you search. If you click on the Cached link, the back-up page will appear as it did on the date it was archived and you will see your key word terms highlighted. The cached link will be missing for sites that have not been indexed, as well as for sites whose owners have requested that Google not cache their content.

Third Line: Similar pages follows the word, Cached, on the third line. Clicking on this link will bring up more sites that are similar. This is a valuable tool.

7.2.7. Prepare A Bibliography File

Look back at Task 4 for illustrations of Bibliography files taken from the Internet. In Illustration 7.2 below you can identify the author, Web title, publisher and the URL.

Illustration 7.2. Bibliographic Data Located For File

7.2.8. Prepare A Note File

Getting notes into your Note file from the Internet is easier than taking notes from print materials. You can search the Internet, locate sources, and take notes anywhere you have access to a computer or a mobile device such as an iPhone, Palm, or Blackberry. It is a good idea to download, print, or Bookmark any sites you will be using because some sites change or disappear over time.

Read the material carefully. When you find good information that relates to your Thesis Question, highlight it in preparation for moving it to your Note file. For example, this site has information describing the Democratic Party's reaction to the Civil War draft.

Illustration 7.3. below shows how you might highlight information you want to use in this Web site.

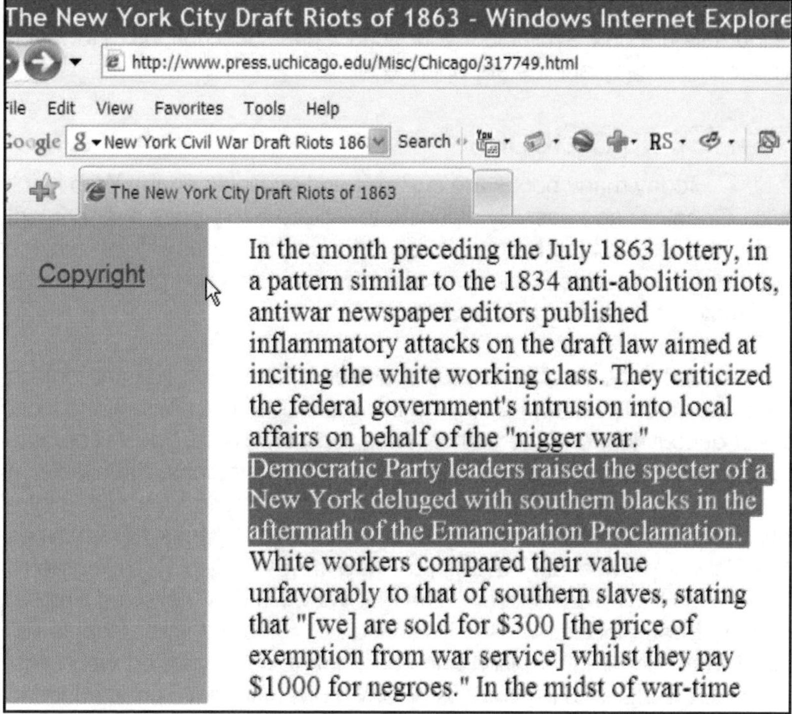

Illustration 7.3. Information Highlighted in Web site.

Look back at Task 5. Review the instructions in Section 5.3. Taking Notes From Internet Sources. Open a new Note file and save it as Harris, the author of the work on the Internet site. Complete all steps 1-9 on page 5-8. In this case you might have copy-pasted the highlighted material you were seeking about the Democratic Party and the Civil War as a direct quotation.

Continue examining each site on the first results page to look for more relevant sites. Click on the Similar pages links that seem relevant to see more pages.

7.3. Google Scholar

Google offers enhanced searching through its Google Scholar engine that limits searching to scholarly works rather than the broad, open Internet. With Scholar you can search peer-reviewed articles in scholarly journals, research papers, theses, abstracts, books and articles published by universities, publishers, academic organizations and other scholarly groups. Moreover, Scholar may be able to help you find relevant articles in your college or university library. Some articles in scholarly journals are only available if your school has subscriptions. However, abstracts of many articles are open to all.

7.4. Google Books

Today many books are digitized and available on the Web in full text. Google is aggressively planning to digitize every book ever printed! If you are researching history, literary criticism, art, or any other subject, you can go to Google Books and probably find many rich print resources that may not be available in your library.

Just type the title, author or subject of the book you are looking for in the search box and Google will find the book or books. If the work is out of copyright or if the author has given permission, you will be able to download a PDF file of the full text including illustrations, if available. If still covered by copyright, Google will present a Limited View with a synopsis of the book and possibly sections of some pages. Sometimes Google will provide only a Snippet View that will display bibliographic information like a card catalog. The Full View, Limited View, and Snippet View will each include a Find This Book In A Library link. Google will include additional information such as book reviews, related web sites, reference works, and illustrations. Many magazines have been added to the PDF collection as well.

7.5. Internet Public Library http://www.ipl.org

The Internet Public Library is a public service organization that is hosted today by Drexel University's College of Information Science & Technology. Type Internet Public Library in the Google search box. You will see a list of the various collections including Humanites, Business, Education, Humanities, Health, Law & Government, Science, Social Science, Reference Works, Encyclopedias, Magazines, Newspapers, LIterary Criticism, and U. S.Presidents, Computers, Science Fair, Business, and Special Collections.

7.6. Digital Object Identifier System (DOI)

The DOI system is a relatively new way of identifiying information. In some ways it is similar to a URL and to the ISBN book numbering system. DOI names can be used to identify any resource including physical and digital products, performances and abstract works. They may be text, audio, or images. Before long most works will be identified with a DOI. DOI names can be used by Internet browsers, too.

All DOI numbers begin with the number 10 followed by a period, a four number prefix, a slash, and a suffix consisting of a string of numbers and or letters.

Here's how a DOI will appear in an APA citation:

Von Ledebur, S.C. (2007). Optimizing knowledge transfer. *Knowledge Management Research and Practice*. Advance online publication. doi:10.1057/palgrave.kmrp.8500141

The American Psychological Association requires citing DOIs in its bibliography References lists if they are assigned to works.

7.6. What About Wikipedia

Wikipedia is an online encyclopedia with each entry a compilation of online contributors who may or may not be experts or scholars. Anyone with access to the Internet can post an entry. Entries are edited collaboratively using software called "wiki," hence its name.

Now that you are aware of its makeup can you trust Wikipedia to be accurate? The answer is yes and no. It certainly is up to date with information on people and events that are in the news now. A recent comparison survey of forty-two entries on scientific subjects in the journal *Nature* found four errors in Wikipedia versus three in Britannica, so it appears to be fairly accurate.

Although Wikipedia is an excellent source for a quick overview of a subject it still does not carry the imprimitur of a truly scholarly research publisher. You should not use its articles in your research. However, Wikipedia can help you locate other valuable sources because it often lists bibliographic entries.

Task 8

Search Online Databases

Task 8: Search Online Databases

Time for Task 8: 3-4 Hours

8.1. Online Databases Defined

It's time to search online databases. This search may be your most productive. If you are wondering what a database is, think of an old-fashioned print Encyclopedia Britannica with its many bound volumes sitting on a shelf in the library. That is a print database. Now imagine that the entire collection has been transformed with every entry squeezed into an electronic file. Virtually any collection of data that is in an electronic file for easy retrieval is called a database.

8.1.1. What Do Online Databases Contain?

Databases contain articles from journals, magazines, and newspapers as well as abstracts or summaries of articles. Full text books, conference proceedings, scholarly articles, research reports, literary research and criticism, book reviews, biographical information, business references, as well as general and specific reference works are available in databases.

Some databases are specialized by subject. For example, you may find a database with information only about the Civil War or Alternative Medicine.

8.1.2. Who Publishes Databases?

Several commercial companies such as Ebsco, ProQuest, Infotrac, GaleNet, Newsbank, SIRS, Project Muse and Grolier are popular database providers. Government agencies, universities, colleges, and scholarly institutions have also developed databases on specific subjects. Many journal and magazine publishers maintain their own databases.

Listed on the next page are a few of the more popular commercial databases you may encounter.

GaleNet - Access World News provides full-text content from over 1500 newspapers, broadcast transcripts and newswires.

InfoTrac Academic OneFile - provides full-text peer-reviewed articles from more than 10,000 journals and reference sources.

InfoTrac General OneFile - offers full-text articles from over 8000 magazines, journals, newspapers and newswires.

New York Times - provides coverage from 1851 to today, with many years available as exact cover-to-cover digital reproductions, and full text coverage from 1995 to present.

Wall Street Journal - offers full text articles from the Wall Street Journal, from 1984 to present.

ProQuest - provides access to many current periodicals and newspapers.

NewsBank - provides full text newspapers.

Ebsco - offers full text magazines and journals.

Project Muse - offers four hundred journals in humanities and social sciences.

8.1.3. Advantages of Online vs. Print Databases

1. Print databases are only updated periodically, usually monthly, semi-annually, or annually. Online databases are continually updated as new information becomes available.

2. Online databases from other libraries or commercial vendors may be retrieved from your library terminal or your own computer via the Internet.

"The Catch"

Most college and secondary school libraries cannot afford to subscribe to all the databases of all possible vendors. Library staffs select those databases they believe will be of most value to their students or card holders. So don't be surprised if you cannot find the specific database you want.

However, if you access your city, county, and state library you will generally find a more comprehensive list of databases available.

8.2. Access Your Library's Online Databases

Open your library's home page at a library terminal or from you own computer. No two library home pages are alike, but look for a link to Online Resources or Databases. In almost all cases you will need a user name and password and/or your library card number.

Identify the databases your library offers. Open those related to your subject to see what they offer. Illustration 8.1 below is an example of one library's link to its databases. These are arranged by subject with several databases available in General Articles, Social Studies, Literature and Arts, Science and Health, Reference.

General Articles	Social Studies	Literature & Arts	Science & Health	Reference
ProQuest Direct	ABC-CLIO Social Studies	Oxford English Dictionary (OED) Online	Science Direct	Oxford English Dictionary (OED) Online
Lexis-Nexis Scholastic	AP Images	ARTstor NOTE: Allow pop-ups.	Discovering Collection: Science	Encyclopedia Americana
JSTOR Periodicals	PsychArticles - full text	Twayne's Authors Series	Health and Wellness Resource Center	World Book Online
N Y Times Historical Archive	Discovering Collection: History	Contemporary Literary Criticism Select	AccessScience	World Book Advanced
AP Images	Business and Company Resource Center	Dictionary of Literary Biography	PsychArticles - full text	Multi-Media Encyclopedia
Project Muse	Columbia International Affairs: CIAO	Lit Finder	New Book of Popular Science	The New Book of Knowledge

Illustration 8.1 A Typical Online Resources Page

8.3. Database Searching

Databases use search engines similar to Google's. Just follow the prompts, enter your search terms, and analyze the results. You will need to use the database's operators and your best key words to get the best search results.

Let's assume that your Thesis Question is How can the U.S. develop a universal health care program that is privately funded? You find that you can access InfoTrac Academic OneFile database from your library. You enter the key words, Health Care Reform in the search box as shown below in Illustration 8.2. below. Other databases will function in a similar fashion.

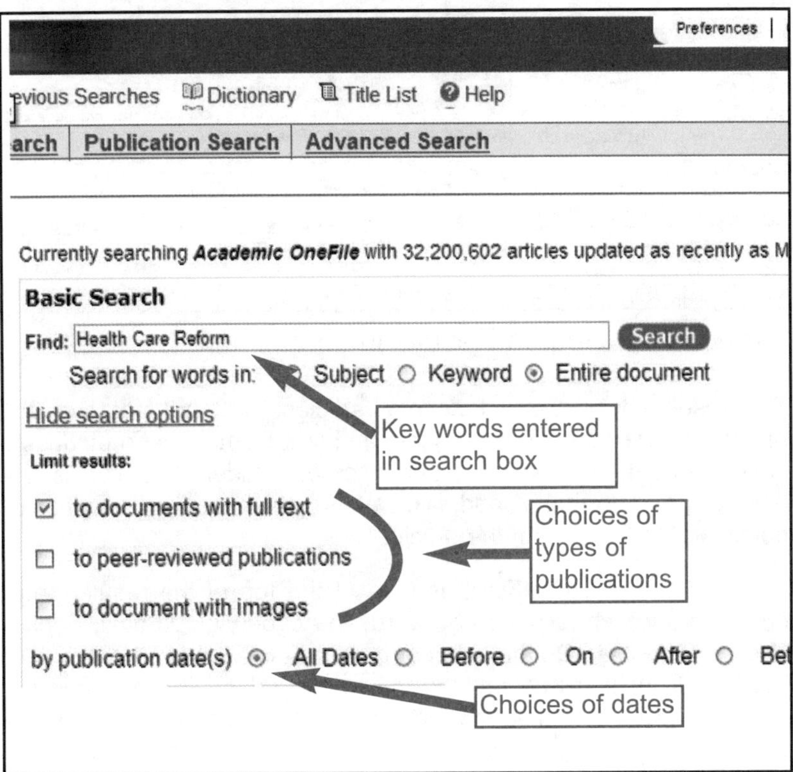

Illustration 8.2. Basic Search Box of Academic OneFile

Note that you are given options to narrow the search to documents with full text, peer reviewed publications, documents with images, and by publication dates.

Documents with full text and All Dates has been selected.

Clicking on the search button yields the screen shown in Illustration 8.3. on the next page.

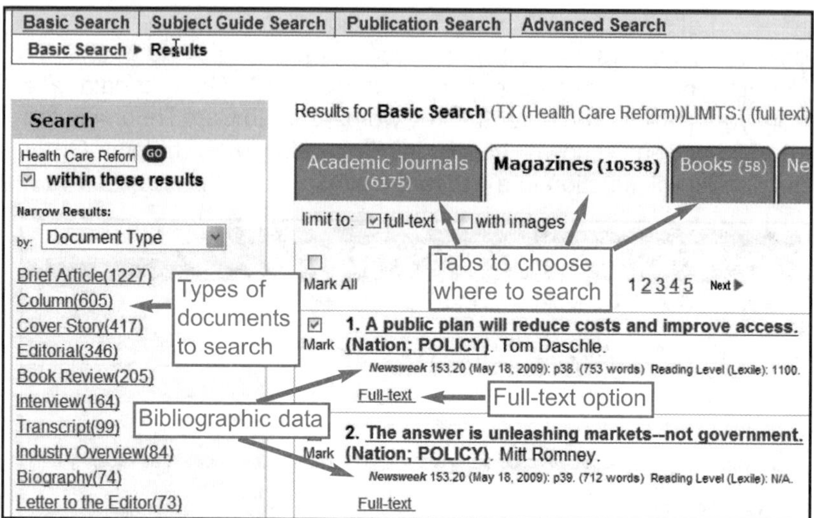

Illustration 8.3 Search Results in Magazines

The results page yielded several articles, but the first two are magazine articles by Tom Daschle and Mitt Romney who obviously have different viewpoints on health care. Under each title is the bibliographic information and a link offering the searcher the option of obtaining the Full-text of the article.

Academic OneFile has tabs at the top of the results page offering to search for your key words in Academic Journals, Books, News and Media. On the side bar to the left is a list of other types of documents including columns, cover stories, editorials, book reviews, interviews, etc. in which Academic OneFile will search for your key words. Other databases will offer similar but different search options.

For purposes of this example, let's assume you want to use the Romney article found under the Magazines tab.

8.4. Prepare a Bibliography File

The author is Mitt Romney, the title of the article is "The Answer Is Unleashing Markets-Not Government." It appeared on page 39 in *Newsweek* magazine on May 18, 2009.

You have all the data you need to prepare a bibliography file. Look back at Task 4 for instructions. You know the drill. You have to look in Chapter 16 if using the MLA for the correct form for an entry from a database.

Hint: the sample is on page 16-14. Note that because articles in online databases may not be exactly as they were in print form, the MLA requires the addition of the name of the database in italics, the medium, Web, and the date of access at the end of the standard entry for a magazine article. If you had read the article in the print magazine, the entry would end with the word, Print, instead of Web after the name of the database.

Don't peek at Illustration 8.4 below. Type the entry in your practice Bibliography file using the information in Illustration 8.3. Then compare your work with that in Illustration 8.4.

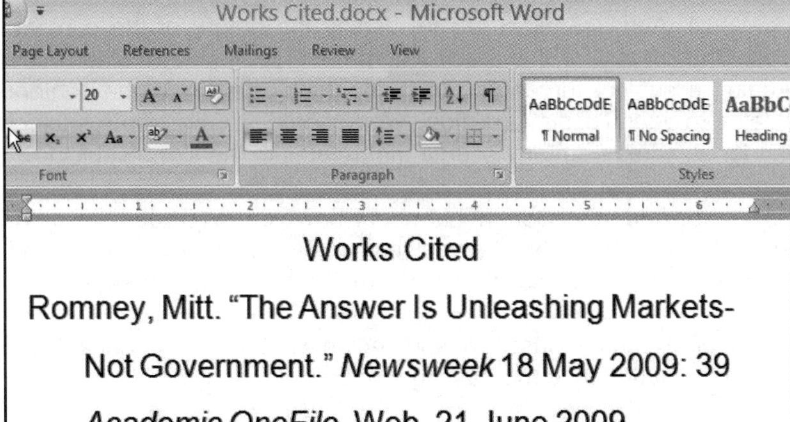

Illustration 8.4. Bibliography File Entry For A Database

The APA and Turabian use different forms. Check the sample entries in Chapters 17 and 18 to be certain of the correct citation if you are using those styles.

8.5. Prepare a Note File

Database note taking is the same as Internet note taking. Let's try to retrieve this article in the database you are using. Always click on the Full Text option if available to see the entire magazine article. If you can retrieve the article, read it and select the sections that you think are appropriate for your hypothetical paper and highlight them. If you can't find this article, try for another one in the databases available to you. Now we can practice preparing a Note file based on the article.

Review the instructions for taking notes from the Internet that follow.

1. Open the Note file and save it with the author's name.

2. Enter the minimum bibliographical data necessary to tie the note to its Bibliography file. You can copy-paste any significant bibliographic data from the database site directly to the Note file. If pages or paragraphs are numbered on the site, be sure to include them in the Note file.

3. Minimize the database site.

4. Add a Subject tag to identify the nature of the content. Your Subject tag for this article might be: Romney - His State Plan. Adding a subject forces you to really think about how the content relates to your Thesis Question. You should use the same subject tag for all notes from any source that relates to the same subject.

5. Add your Comments about how you might use the data, about any questions the piece raises, or your reaction to it. Here you might type: How successful is Romney Plan in Massachusetts?

6. Read the passage. and decide whether you will lift a direct quotation, summarize the passage, or paraphrase it.

7. Copy-paste the material into your Note file.

8. Change the font and color of the material.

9. Save the file and move the it into the My Document Note folder.

You have prepared several practice Note files so you should be very proficient and confident.

Continue your search in all available and appropriate databases. For example, researching the Thesis Question How can the U.S. develop a universal health care program that is privately funded? you might find good material in the social studies, health, government, or medical association databases.

Task 9

Develop Your Thesis Statement

Task 9: Develop Your Thesis Statement

Time for Task 8: 3 Hours

9.1. Review Your Preliminary Research

In Task 2 you developed a Thesis Question. You should now have at least five to ten good sources in your Bibliography and Note files from your physical library search, your Internet search, and your database search.

Open your Note folder. Carefully and critically re-read each of your Note files. What are the points of view? Are there agreements and disagreements? Are there major controversies? Do some notes provide support for ideas in the form of statistics or the comment of an authority? Is there a special area of your Thesis Question that interests you? Have you discovered cause and effect relationships? Is information lacking on some aspect of the question? Do you have a clearer idea of the significant issues? You should be able to identify and articulate the major points of your Thesis Question.

Print your Note files and organize them by your Subject tags. For example, if your Thesis Question is How Did Slavery Affect Political Parties? you might have several items with Democratic Party Subject tags and several with Republican Party Subject tags. There might be some with Democratic Party-Irish tags or some with Republican Party-Indian Problems tags.

Go back to the prewriting exercises described in Task 2 and do them again, this time with your research information. Set the material aside for a day to let the ideas percolate in your mind. This is the most important part of the research paper project because it will lead to the writing of your THESIS STATEMENT.

9.2. Develop Your Thesis Statement

After you have reviewed your preliminary research and redone the pre-writing exercises you must develop a Thesis Statement that can be "proved" or supported by your paper. Your Thesis Statement should be a declarative sentence.

Several different approaches can be used to develop your Thesis Statement. Just below is a chart labeled Thesis Approaches. Study each approach carefully. Decide how you want to frame your final thesis.

THESIS APPROACHES	
Chronology---	The rise of the Imagist Movement can be traced over a period of twenty years.
Procedure---	Five steps are required to produce liquid oxygen.
Cause/Effect---	Economic factors caused deterioration in Sino-Soviet relations in 1950.
Problem---	Differing Moslem ideologies make Israeli-Palestinian peace difficult.
Solution---	The energy crisis can be solved by solar and nuclear power.
Comparison---	Acupuncture is a better anesthetic than malothane.
Similarity---	TV and motion picture writing are similar in several respects.
Difference---	Marriage rites differ among Far Eastern, Middle Eastern and Western fami lies.
Relationship---	Hemingway's life experiences influenced his work.
Analysis---	Three major issues are related to the crisis in North Korea.
Literary Theme---	Romanticism embodies strong conceptions of scientific ideas of the Classical period.
Pro---	Kennedy's handling of the Cuban missile crisis was good foreign policy.
Con---	Four research studies disprove value of low fat diets in reducing heart attacks.
Category---	Several ethnic populations in America grew during the past ten years.

For example, if you want to prove that socio-economic class is related to school failure you will be using a "cause-effect" approach. If you want to prove that Obama's handling of the

Afghanistan situation was good foreign policy, you will be using a "pro" approach. Your emerging Thesis Statement should be based on one of the approaches listed.

9.2.1. Write Trial Thesis Statements

Write some trial declarative Thesis Statements based on your original Thesis Question. For example, if your original Thesis Question in the area of criminal justice is:

How effective are boot camps in reducing recidivism?

You might simply turn that into a Cause and Effect Thesis Statement such as:

Boot camps are effective in reducing recidivism

or, if your research seemed to prove otherwise:

Boot camps are not effective in reducing recidivism

or you might take a "pro" position with:

Boot camps reduce costs of youth incarceration

or if your research seemed to prove otherwise you might decide on a "con" approach:

Boot camps increase costs of youth incarceration

Be sure your thesis is significant and worth the effort you are putting into it. The Thesis Statement should be about a situation, concern, or idea that is controversial, timely, and debatable.

9.2.2. Use The Thesis Statement Checklist

Identify which thesis approach you are using. Think the words, "I believe..." just before you write your Thesis Statement. This will insure that YOU and YOUR ideas are in the paper. Check your Thesis Statement against the Thesis Statement Checklist on the next page.

If your Thesis Statement meets all the criteria on the Checklist, go on to Task 10. If not, go through the steps of Task 9 again and write a new Thesis Statement.

THESIS CHECKLIST

My Thesis Statement is:

(I believe) ______________________________

____

My Thesis Statement:

- ▶ uses the (select from the list above) thesis approach.
- ▶ is not too broad.
- ▶ is not too narrow or technical unless required.
- ▶ can be proved with the material I have found.
- ▶ is scholarly.
- ▶ is OK with my instructor.

Task 10

Write Your Outline

Task 10: Write Your Outline

Time for Task 8: 2 Hours

10.1. Develop An Outline From Your Thesis Statement

It is time to plan how you will write your paper and prove your Thesis Statement. The outline is the plan. You cannot write a satisfactory paper without one.

An outline is like a road map. To prove your Thesis Statement you have to plan the route from beginning to end. You want your readers to know what you believe about your thesis and you want to show them all the data you have gathered to prove it.

How do you draw your road map? Think about how you can best prove your Thesis Statement. Imagine yourself a lawyer who has to prove his or her case to a jury. How can you arrange your arguments one after the other to build your case? How can you summarize and clinch your arguments? Your answers to these questions will suggest the topics and sub-topics of your outline.

10.2. Outline Styles

There are two popular outline styles in current use:

The Harvard outline style
The decimal outline style

Outline Styles

Harvard Outline	Decimal Outline
I.	1.
A.	1. 1.
B.	1. 2.
1.	1. 2. 1.
2.	1. 2. 2.
a.	1.2.2.1
b.	1.2.2.2
c.	1.2.2.3

When you write your outline be sure that Main Topics shown by the roman numerals I. and II. in the Harvard outline or arabic 1. and 2. in the decimal outline have the same level of importance.

Sub-topics A and B in the Harvard outline should be of equal importance and support the main topic I. The sub-topics 1.1. and 1.2. in the decimal outline should be of equal importance and support main topic 1.

An outline is considered faulty if it contains only one sub-topic under a main topic. Thus, the outline below is not correct because there is only one sub-topic under main topic 1. and only one sub-topic under 2.2.

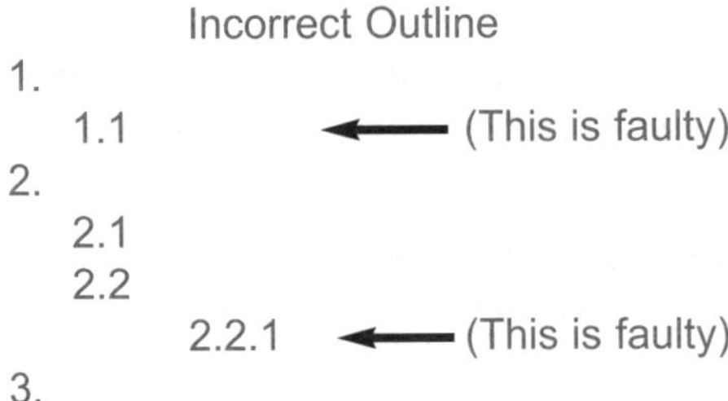

10.3. Sentence Outline

Use complete sentences for each topic and sub-topic. These topic sentences will head your paragraphs.

Let's assume your Thesis Statement is:

Global Warming Affects The U.S. Economy

Pretend you have collected many Note files and you found information about the ways climate is affecting businesses and the ways businesses are responding.

10.4. Check and Print All Your Note Files

You would have several Note files from your searches in the physical library, on the Internet, and in databases. Then you would have checked to be sure that every Note file has the following data:

1. Minimum bibliographic information including author and, title to link the Note file to its corresponding Bibliography file including a call number, library location, or Internet URL so you can retrieve it for further information if needed.
2. Your Subject tag showing how the Note relates to your Thesis Statement.
3. Your Comments about the source.
4. A quotation, summary, paraphrase or raw material.

Then, you would print out all of your Note files.

10.5. Arrange Note Files To Develop Your Outline

The next step would be to study your Note files to see how you could use them to prove your Thesis Statement. Remember, you must prepare your case for the jury!

You would first write a main topic sentence to open the arguments with some evidence to prove Global Warming Affects the U. S. Economy.

Pretend you found evidence that

Global warming affects U.S. businesses.
and
Businesses respond in several ways.

These would be the first two main topics that would begin to prove your Thesis Statement.

Assume that as you sorted through your Note files, you found five separate ways that Global warming affects U.S. businesses, your first topic sentence. These five would be sub-topics under that main topic sentence.

Assume that you found two major methods businesses are using to respond to global warming. These two would be sub-topics under the second main topic sentence.

Your outline would be beginning to take shape. You would continue the process, drafting main topics first, adding the sub-topics and sub-sub-topics.

You would match each Note file to its related topic and sub-topic sentence deciding how you could use the authority statements, statistics, illustrations, or other material you found to back up your topics and sub-topics.

When finished, your hypothetical outline might look like the one on page 10-6. Type the outline below as shown in Illustration 10.1. for practice. There wasn't room in the illustration for topic 2.2., but include it in your practice Outline. Double space each topic and sub-topic sentence.

Global Warming Affects the U.S. Economy

1. Global warming affects U.S. businesses

    1.1. Health care costs increase because of climate changes.

    1.2. Energy costs increase due to need for greater cooling.

    1.3. Property insurance premiums increase because of storm damage.

    1.4. Waterway transportation costs increase because of reduced river flow.

    1.5. Agricultural businesses lose because of changing grow ing seasons.

2. Businesses respond in several ways.

    2.1. Businesses reduce dependence on fossil fuel.

        2.1.1. Solar voltaic cells save 40-80% in costs.

        2.1.2. Wind power provides substantial power.

        2.1.3. Biomass power is successfully used.

    2.2. Businesses reconstruct or modify buildings.

        2.2.1. Plants are built to different standards.

        2.2.2. Power plants are using modern technology.

        2.2.3. Businesses install energy efficient equipment.

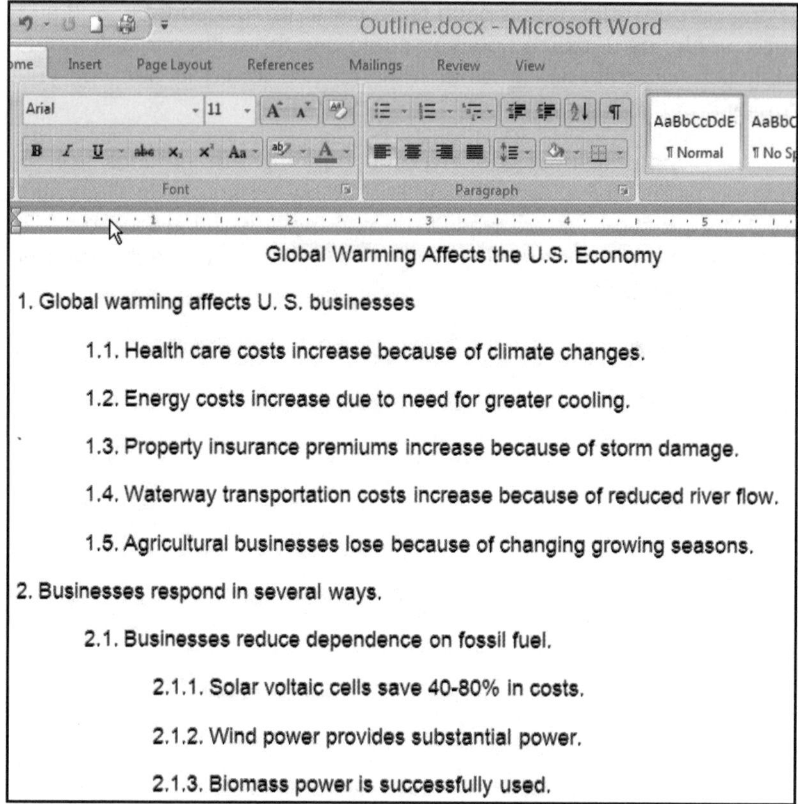

Illustration 10.1. Outline File in Microsoft Word

10.6. OPEN YOUR OUTLINE FILE

Now you will prepare an outline for your own Thesis Statement. Open a new file and save it as Outline. Follow the procedures in 10.4. and 10.5. When you prepare your own outline, you may find that some Note files are not as relevant to your Thesis Statement as you had originally thought or you may want to change some Subject tags. You may also find that more information is needed to support some topics or sub-topics, so you will have to do more searching. Check to be sure your outline is not faulty. A topic with only one supporting sub-topic makes your outline improper. If you find such an error, go back and re-work the outline.

Take a good look when you are finished. Are all the main topics of equal importance? Do the sub-topics support the main topics. Are the sub-topics of equal importance? If you are satisfied with your outline, you can proceed to Task 11. where you will learn how to flesh out your outline and put some meat on its bones.

Task 11

Flesh Out Your Outline

Task 11: Flesh Out Your Outline

Time for Task 11: 2 Hours

11.1. Download Note Files to Outline File

Now you will paste the quotations, paraphrases, summaries, in your Note files directly under the related topic and sub-topic sentences in your Outline file. Let's see how this is done. In Task 10 we wrote an outline for the Thesis Statement Global Warming Affects the U.S. Economy.

Assume your research led you to a good Web site as shown below in Illustration 11.1.

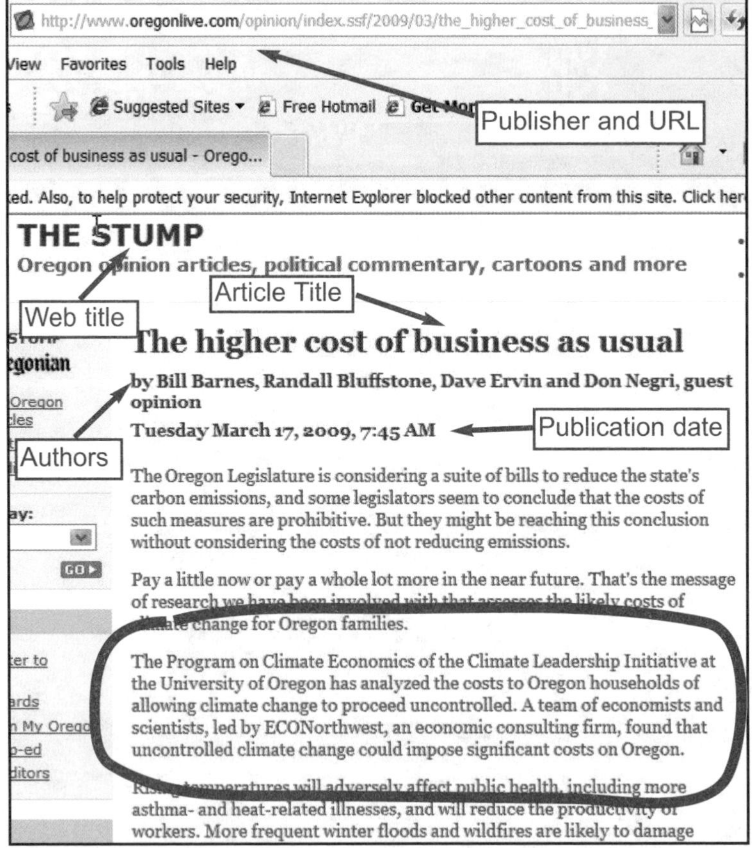

Illustration 11.1. Web site Global Warming-Business

You had all the data for a Bibliography file: the authors, the article title, the Web title, the publisher, the URL, and the publication date. These are shown in Illustration 11.1. So pretend you prepared a Bibliography file. You are an expert at Bibliography files now.

As you read through the Web page, you learned that a team of economists and scientists found that climate change would cost Oregon businesses dearly. The passage is shown circled in Illustration 11.1.

Assume that you prepared a Barnes Note file and pasted the quotation into it as shown in Illustration 11.2. below.

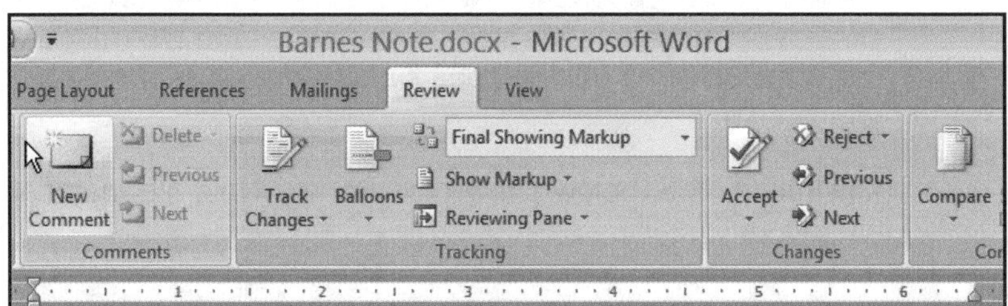

Bill Barnes, Randall Bluffstone, Dave Ervin and Don Negri

"The Higher Cost of Business as Usual"'

http://www.oregonlive.com/opinion/index.ssf/2009/03/the_higher_cost_of_business_as.html

SUBJECT: Climate change will bring high costs to Oregon

COMMENTS: Oregon sees it coming. What about US Govt.?

QUOTATION

"A team of economists and scientists, led by ECONorthwest, an economic consulting firm, found that uncontrolled climate change could impose significant costs on Oregon."

Illustration 11.2. Note file Oregon Web site.

As you organized all of your printed Note files by topic and sub-topic in your outline, you noted that this statement from a recognized authority supports your first topic sentence, Global warming affects U.S. businesses.

Now you want to move the material in this Note file directly into your Outline file.

Here's how to do it:

1. Open your Barnes Note file and your Outline file.

2. Copy-paste the material you want to insert under the topic sentence in your Outline file. Be sure the pasted material is in a distinctive font and color to differentiate it from your own writing.

3. Copy-paste the authors' names into the Outline file under the quoted material. Later, when adding a parenthetical citation or endnote in the text of your paper you will refer to the corresponding Bibliography file for detailed information if you need it.

Illustration 11.3. below shows the Barnes Note file material pasted into the Outline file.

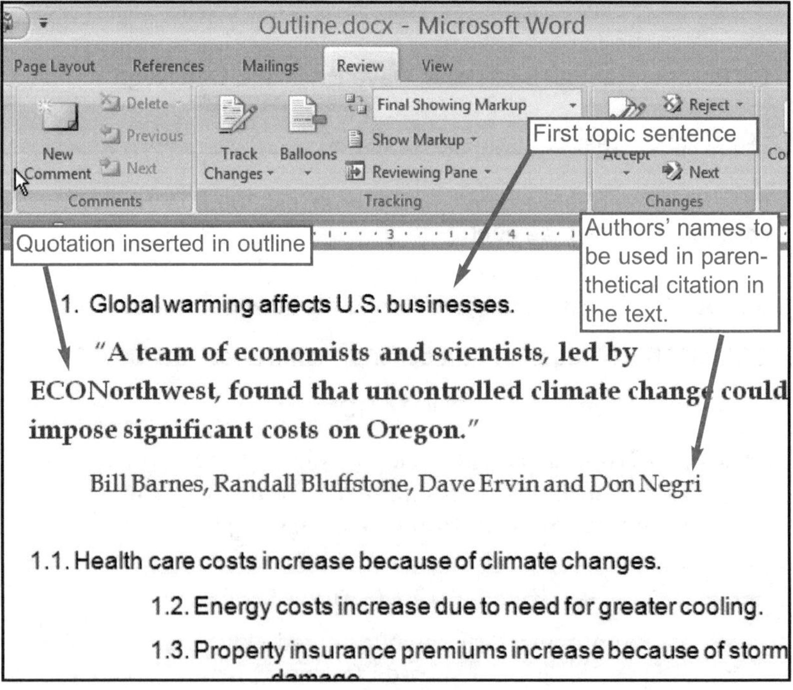

Illustration 11.3. Note File Material Pasted Into Outline

Now you have material from one Note file under the first topic sentence. You may or may not need need to add more. You decide.

You would continue the process until all topics and sub-topics have sufficient note material under each. Now you know how to download material from your Note files into your Outline file.

11.2. Avoid Just Cutting and Pasting

You have finished researching in the library, on the Internet and in databases. You have many Note files, but you certainly want to do more than just cut and paste the work of others. You have gathered the material to prove ***your*** Thesis Statement.

You must use your research as the basis for your own arguments. Your goal is to incorporate the quotations, paraphrases, and summaries of your sources into a coherent, unified, and logical document marked by powerful, effective, and outstanding writing. Your language is paramount. You should use your research material to bolster what you write.

In Task 12 you will study the Writing Process and learn to prepare a literate, intelligently crafted research paper. Learning how to use the writing process will give you another tool to help you in the creation of your paper. You will learn how to build powerful, organized paragraphs and to weave them together in an organized fashion.

You will gain new knowledge of how to vary sentence openings and sentence lengths to improve your writing style and how to eliminate wordiness to make your writing crisp and accurate. Finally, you will learn about the dangers of plagiarism and how to protect yourself.

You are nearing the end of this journey to the completion of an outstanding paper!

Task 12

The Writing Process

Task 12: The Writing Process

Time for Task 12: 1-2 Hours

Now that you have inserted all of the passages, quotations, paraphrases, and summaries from your Note files into your Outline file, you are ready to begin writing the first draft of your paper. Writing requires time and effort to produce a good product. The process includes preparing several drafts so you can sharpen and improve your paper.

Your outline with its source material inserted is the skeleton of your paper. The next step is to merge the material in your outline with your own writing to create a paper that is well-written and highly readable. The primary structure of all writing is the paragraph, so let's begin with a brief review of the makings of powerful paragraphs.

12.1. Paragraphs - The Writing Building Block

Paragraphs are the building blocks of a great piece of writing. A good paragraph starts off with a topic sentence somewhere near its beginning followed by a series of supporting sentences.

Topic Sentences

The topic sentence sends a signal letting your reader know what is coming. Think of the topic sentence as the battle flag of a platoon of soldier ideas that follow. The topic sentence should be about a single idea. Topic sentences do not always have to be the first sentence, but they should appear near the beginning of the paragraph.

All of your topic and sub-topic sentences are already in your Outline document so you are ready to go. As you write you may realize that there may be a better way of expressing some of your topic sentences, so feel free to change any that you think could be improved.

Unity

Good paragraphs have unity which means that paragraphs should be about one unified idea. Every sentence must add some information related to and supporting the topic sentence. Be on the lookout for extraneous or stray ideas that have nothing to do with the topic sentence and get rid of them.

Coherence

The definition of "cohere" is to stick together. A paragraph has coherence when the sentences stick together in an organized fashion. You want your reader to understand the paragraph by reading sentences that are related and expand on the topic sentence. Different types of supporting sentences help to make your paragraphs coherent.

Logic

Good paragraphs are developed logically, requiring you to state your topic sentence and arrange the supporting sentences in logical order. There should be no rambling or diversions. Think of the logic of your argument before you begin to write and be certain your sentences are logically connected to prove your point.

12.1.1. Use Supporting Sentences To Achieve Unity, Coherence, And Logic

Supporting sentences insure that your paragraphs have unity, coherence, and logic. Types of supporting sentences are described below.

Explanation

An explanatory sentence tries to give the reader more information about the topic sentence making the idea clearer, simpler, and easier to grasp. Explanations elucidate the original topic sentence and give the reader a better understanding of its point. Opening an explanatory sentence with a phrase such as "By way of explanation ..." prepares your reader for an explanatory sentence.

Example

These sentences give the reader an example of a concept or idea in your topic sentence. Simply stating "For example..." to begin a sentence containing an example alerts your reader to subconsciously look back at the topic sentence, digest it, and prepare for the example that is coming.

Contrast

Using a concept better known to your reader that is different or even opposite from the one you are writing about helps the reader see your original idea more clearly. Opening with a phrase such as "On the other hand..." or "An opposing view..." lets your reader know that a contrasting idea is on the way.

Comparison

Comparing the idea of your topic sentence with a similar idea, perhaps more familiar to your reader, helps to clarify the original idea. You might begin your comparison sentence with such a phrase as "In comparison..."

Illustration

Illustrative sentences use details to describe a point about your topic sentence. They tend to be a bit longer because you want to draw a detailed word picture to illustrate what you are trying to describe. Simply stating, "To illustrate..." alerts your reader that an illustration follows.

Statistics

Statistical information can bolster your topic sentence argument by adding numerical data that proves and bolsters the point you are making. Beginning a sentence with a phrase such as "Statistics from the report of..." leads the reader to get set to do some math. Statistics can substantially support a topic sentence idea by providing mathematical proof.

Authority

Using the words of a scholar, a person of authority such as a government official, or a person who has personal experience can add powerful support to your topic sentence. Authority sentences might be introduced with a phrase such as "No less an authority than..."

Chronology

Some paragraphs are developed around a chronology. If you are describing a series of events over time, it is appropriate to use sentences introduced by words such as "First...," or "Later in the century...," or "By the fifth month...," These introductory words help your reader follow the chronology you are reporting.

Summary

After carefully crafting your paragraph, bring the paragraph to a close by summing up the ideas and showing how the paragraph supports the topic sentence. Your topic sentence told your readers what you were going to say. The summary reiterates the point. Stating, "In summary...," to introduce your final sentence leads the reader to mentally review all that has been written in that paragraph.

12.1.2. How To Use Supporting Sentences

The various supporting sentences should be logically arranged to best support the topic sentence. However, do not slavishly follow a formula building every paragraph with the same series of explanations, examples, contrasts, comparisons, illustrations, statistics, and authority. Rather select sentences that best support the topic sentence. For example, you might first use an explanation immediately after your topic sentence. An example of that explanation might logically follow. A comparison sentence might then follow. An illustration of the comparison could be next. Your next paragraph would probably use an entirely different assortment of supporting sentences.

Sample Paragraph

Look at the sample paragraph in the box on the next page. Each of the sentences is labeled so you can see how each sentence is used to support the topic sentence. The paragraph passes the Unity test because every sentence is about ethanol. There are no sentences about other matters. It passes the Coherence test because every sentence supports the main idea. The last sentence summarizes virtually everything in the paragraph. Finally, the paragraph is logically developed with the supporting sentences arranged in logical order and It ends with a strong summary statement.

Of course, the tags would not be typed in a regular paragraph. It would appear as one single paragraph without the indenting and the tags.

12.2. Improving Writing Style

Many papers are spoiled by immature sentence development. Beginning writers are intent on avoiding sentence fragments and run-on sentences, so they overuse a subject - verb pattern. For example, a novice might write sentences like these:

Global warming is a fact.
Carbon dioxide causes environmental damage.
Cars send pollutants into the air.

Although grammatically correct, over use of the subject-verb form leads to boring writing. By varying sentence openings you can vitalize your writing and make your reader excited about your subject. Here's how to do it:

Unity, Coherence, and Logical Organization in a Sample Paragraph about Ethanol

Topic Sentence - Ethanol is being touted as the best alternative to gasoline to help the United States free itself from its gasoline addiction and dependence on Middle Eastern countries.

Explanation - Ethanol is produced by fermenting crops that grow in abundance in the United States.

Example - For example, wheat, barley and corn are used as are the "cellulosic biomass" plants such as trees and wild grasses that are widely available.

Illustration - To illustrate, ethanol is easily blended with gasoline in proportions of 85% ethanol and 15% gasoline to produce E85, a fuel that is currently in use in many Flexible Fuel Vehicles. These vehicles are affordable and increasingly popular.

Authority - The U.S. Environmental Protection Agency also points out that E85 reduces greenhouse gas emissions and other air pollutants.

Summary - Ethanol can not only reduce our demand for oil, but also provide another market for corn thus helping the agricultural industry.

12.2.1. Vary Sentence Openings

Use some of these openings:

Single Word Modifiers: adjectives or adverbs.
Phrases: groups of words with neither a subject or predicate.
Clauses: groups of words with subjects and predicates.

Single Word Modifiers

Nervously, he walked to the podium.

Disgusted, Mary turned and walked away.

Prepositional Phrases

After the test, the subjects left.
With brown stains, the coats looked awful.
Down with taxes was the party's war cry.

Present Participial Phrases

Walking quickly, the group left.
Standing alone, the painting was beautiful.
Writing a term paper is not easy.

Past Participial Phrases

Exhausted by his efforts, he died.
Overjoyed with the news, Bob jumped up.
Betrayed by his men, the general resigned.

Infinitive Phrases

To avoid arrest, the immigrants fled.
To make a deal, he will do anything.
To live free is a blessing.

Subordinate Clauses

Because the law called for the death penalty, no other verdict was possible.
If the results differ, the careful researcher should examine the procedures.
Although he believed her story, the reporter continued to investigate.
When he attempted to fly the latest model, he lost control of the airplane.
Whether or not he succeeded, it is great that he tried.

12.2.2. Vary Sentence Lengths

Short sentences are excellent to add emphasis or to describe very complicated ideas, but do not overuse them. Add variety by using simple, compound, complex, and compound-complex sentences.

Simple Sentence: One independent clause

The Republican convention takes place in August.

Compound Sentence: Two independent clauses

The project took two months, but the result was worth the wait.

Complex Sentence: An independent and a subordinate clause

When he took the witness stand, we knew he would commit perjury.

Compound-Complex Sentence: Two or more independent and one or more dependent clauses

He expressed no opinion, and when the others disagreed, he adjourned the meeting.

12.2.3. Maintain Verb Tense Consistency

In general, try to maintain the same tense throughout the paper. However, in formal research writing some shifts are acceptable.

Past Tense: Action that took place entirely in the past.

Richardson described his experimental results.

Present Perfect Tense: Action that started in the past but is not terminated.

Richardson has shown that his results proved...

The past and present perfect tense are appropriate for review of research literature or discussion of the work of others. It is also appropriate for describing the results of experiments in APA papers.

Present Tense: Action that takes place in the present.

The results of the investigation indicate...

The present tense is appropriate for discussing results and presenting conclusions in APA papers.

Past Perfect Tense: Action that is completed before another action has begun.

The students had completed all their work before we arrived.

Future Perfect Tense: Action that will begin in the future and end at a specific time in the future.

All of the students will have received their grades by this time tomorrow.

12.2.4. Eliminate Wordiness

1. Change From Passive Voice To Active Voice.

An active voice verb denotes action by the subject.
A passive voice verb denotes action upon the subject.
Active verbs generate power and eliminate extra words.

BAD: **Abraham Lincoln *was confronted* by Stanton.** (6 words)

BETTER: **Stanton *confronted* Abraham Lincoln.** (4 words)

2. Change abstract nouns ending -ion to verbs or verb forms. Nouns are weak. Verbs add energy to your writing.

BAD: **The *continuation* of the *production* of greenhouse gases leads directly to the *destruction* of glaciers.** (16 words)

BETTER: ***Continuing to produce* green house gases *destroys* glaciers.** (8 words)

3. Change prepositional phrases into single adjectives or adverbs.

BAD: **The nations *with democratic governments* have most success.** (8 words)

BETTER: ***Democratic* nations have most success.** (5 words)

4. Change *who, that, which* clauses into single words or phrases.

BAD: **The shuttle Discovery, *which had safety problems that had gone undetected*, took off for space.** (15 words)

BETTER: **The shuttle Discovery took off for space *with undetected safety problems*.** (11 words)

Writing Process

5. Eliminate *which* and *that* altogether if possible.

BAD: **Because the arguments for the defense, *which* were unchallenged, the prosecution team *that* was unprepared lost the case.** (18 words)
BETTER: **Because the defense arguments were unchallenged, the unprepared prosecution team lost the case.** (13 words)

6. Change infinitive phrases into verbs.

BAD: **The purpose of the study was *to test* the hypothesis.** (10 words)
BETTER: **The study *tested* the hypothesis.** (5 words)

7. Eliminate the sentence openings *There are, There is,* and *It is.*

BAD: ***There are* several reasons for the system's failure.** (8 words)
BETTER: **The system failed for several reasons.** (6 words)

8. Join two sentences, especially when the second begins with *this.*

BAD: **Ethanol is increasingly being produced. *This* has reduced the demand for gasoline.** (12 words)
BETTER: **Ethanol is increasingly produced, reducing demand for gasoline.** (9 words)

9. Avoid using common wordy expressions. Use their single word alternatives.

BAD: **owing to, considering the fact, the reason why, due to the fact.**
BETTER: **because, why, since**

BAD: **at this point in time**
BETTER: **now**

BAD: **under the circumstances when, on the occasion of**
BETTER: **when**

BAD: **it is necessary to, it is important that, there is a need to**
BETTER: **must**

BAD: **has the ability to, is able to**
BETTER: **can**

BAD: **it is possible, it may occur, there is the possibility**
BETTER: **could, may**

10. Eliminate redundant words that mean the same as a single word.

BAD: **free gift, referred back, past history, true facts, end result, basic fundamen tals, unexpected surprise, red color**

BETTER: **gift, referred, history, facts, result, fundamentals, surprise, red**

BAD: **point in time, in a confused state, unclean in appearance, extreme degree, rough texture, round in shape.**
BETTER: **point, confused, unclean, extreme, rough, round**

BAD: **various and sundry, full and complete, each and every one**
BETTER: **various, complete, each**

11. Eliminate modifiers of words that logically cannot be modified.

BAD: **more perfect, very unique**
BETTER: **perfect, unique**

12.3. Use Transitions To Tie Paragraphs Together

It is important to link all of your paragraphs together just as you link the sentences within each paragraph. You want to ensure that there is a logical progression from paragraph to paragraph.

You can use the same transitional words and phrases described used to link supporting sentences to link paragraphs. Often, repeating a word, phrase, or term from a preceding paragraph in the opening sentence of the following paragraph is all that is needed to make the transition between paragraphs.

12.4. Unity, Coherence, and Logic In Your Paper

Just as you wrote your paragraphs to have unity, coherence, and logical development, be sure your paper has the same attributes. It must be about one major idea or thesis, the paragraphs must stick together, and the paper must be logically organized. Paragraphs should be joined by appropriate transitions. Apply the the lessons you learned about paragraph development as you write your first draft.

Remember, your goal is to prove your Thesis Statement and it must reflect you and your belief. While you will rely heavily on your research sources, be sure the major thrust of the paper is your own. Keep repeating, "I believe..." about your thesis as you write to be sure you do not just cut and paste the ideas of others into your paper.

Proceed until you have written powerful paragraphs in your Research Paper Document for every topic sentence in your outline. Work straight through to the end.

12.5. Plagiarism

Plagiarism is the use of another author's words or ideas as one's own. Writers must be scrupulous about avoiding plagiarism. The protection of intellectual property has long been a hallmark of the world of words. Both the *MLA Handbook for Writers of Research Papers,* 7th Edition and the *Publication Manual of the APA,* 6th Edition have clearly articulated statements that define plagiarism.

12.5.1. Seriousness of the Issue

Several years ago, no less than a prominent and highly regarded American historian used another writer's work in a book. Although there was an admission of guilt, tempered somewhat by a statement that the plagiarism was inadvertent, the historian lost credibility.

Later, a popular president of a prestigious college resigned after it was found that he had inadvertently used someone else's ideas or words without citing the source in a relatively unimportant speech.

Even the *New York Times* is not immune. Two editors resigned after a reporter's false and plagiarized stories were uncovered. The *Times*, in an effort to re-establish its reputation, published the results of its detailed internal investigation. The newspaper, long regarded as the zenith of journalistic excellence, suffered a tremendous loss of prestige. As you can see, the publishing establishment regards the theft of ideas or words as a serious crime and a significant ethical lapse.

12.5.2. Students and Plagiarism

Students may feel that their situation is different. The research papers they write are usually not for general publication unless they are required theses for academic degrees. Many thousands of papers are assigned annually and students may believe that their writing is unimportant and they should not be held to the same standards as professional writers.

As a student you are learning to write a quality paper. You are researching in the library and on the Internet, gathering facts, evaluating and selecting from many ideas, developing and defending a thesis, improving your thinking skills, and honing your writing talents. You are learning, too, one of the the most basic elements in the history of ideas - the protection of intellectual property.

Tremendous damage is done to student-teacher relationships as well as to the reputations of schools and colleges when plagiarism occurs.

12.5.3. Penalties for Plagiarism

Most institutions have very strict penalties for plagiarism that may have far reaching effects on a student's future. Aside from the personal embarrassment, penalties vary, but may include the following:

1. Failing grade for the paper.
2. Failure of the course.
3. Loss of academic credit.
4. Suspension from school.
5. Expulsion from school.

There can be other losses as well. For example, a student may not receive or may lose a previously granted recommendation for acceptance to a graduate school, college, or job. In addition, there is the very serious loss of credibility by peers, associates, and staff. What statement has the student plagiarist made about his or her character? Are these penalties worth the failure to meet rigorous academic and publishing standards?

12.5.4. Types of Plagiarism

Purchase of Papers

It is easy to find and download research papers on every conceivable topic on the Internet - for a price. Faced with missed deadlines, desperate, dishonest, or lazy students submit such papers whole or use the purchased paper's ideas and language without attribution. This is perhaps the worst form of plagiarism because it is entirely intentional.

Failure to Document Sources

Some students fail to understand that all ideas and the language of others, whether summarized, paraphrased, or quoted, must be acknowledged by a citation. Once you download any material into your outline or your paper, you must be diligent about identifying the author and the source of that material. Care must be taken that during your writing you do not forget that the words, phrases, and ideas you pasted in your Note files and Outline are not your own.

Today there are computer programs available to instructors that can instantly match the words in your paper with the original sources. Many schools use that technology to identify plagiarism. You have been warned.

Accidental Plagiarism Prevention

Beware of accidental plagiarism when inserting your source material into your Research Paper Document. Be absolutely certain that the paraphrases, quotes, and summaries are in an entirely different font from any of your own original sentences because these are not your words or ideas. Here's how to do it.

1. Use Times New Roman or Arial for your own writing. Arial looks like this: These are my words.

2. Highlight the paraphrase, quote, or summary.

3. Click on Format in the Tool Bar and select a font. Book Antiqua looks like this: This is data from one of my sources.

Always use the same font for all of your sources so you will easily differentiate them from your own words as you prepare the first draft. In subsequent drafts you will change the source material font to match your own, but they will be properly cited.

All quotes must be enclosed in quotation marks and cited. Summaries and paraphrases must be cited.

Accidental Plagiarism

Sometimes after researching a topic students will become so engrossed in the subject that they begin to believe that some ideas are really their own and inadvertently fail to give attribution to the original author(s).

Some expressions fall into the realm of "common knowledge." Common knowledge consists of those ideas or expressions that are so widely known that most people use them without knowing their source. Writers may be excused from citing such expressions because they have virtually become part of our language or are unquestionably known to all. Would a writer be faulted for using the expression, "George Washington was the first president of the United States." Absolutely not. However, if you add that as the first president Washington used the veto power granted in the Constitution, you had better tell your reader how you know.

Some common expressions that were originally in a work of poetry, the Bible, or other literary forms have been passed down in our language and are so commonly heard that most people have forgotten or have never known the sources. While some of these may not be examples of plagiarism, it is best to give attribution if you can.

You are using the intellectual work and ideas of others in developing your thesis. Your arguments have been built on your careful research. Why not, then, let everyone know the care you took in research and the scope and depth that you plumbed to reach your conclusions. Be proud of your work and cite your sources.

Be honest and careful. Don't plagiarize!

Task 13

Write The First Draft

Task 13: Write The First Draft

Time for Task 12: 3 Hours

You now know how to build powerful paragraphs and to enhance your writing style by varying sentence openings and sentence lengths and maintaining verb tense consistency. You fleshed out your outline by inserting all of your raw notes, quotations, summaries, and paraphrases under your topic and sub-topic sentences. You have the scoop on plagiarism.

As you write and insert the quotations, paraphrases, and summaries of your sources, you must let your readers know who your sources are and where they can locate the same information. Each of the three handbooks uses different citation styles. You and your instructor may decide which one you will use. It's time to start writing. Let's go!

13.1. Decide Which Citation Style You Will Be Using To Document Your Paper

You have a choice of the *Modern Language Association Handbook,* the *Publication Manual of the American Psychological Association,* or *Turabian - A Manual for Writers of Term Papers, Theses, and Dissertations.* All three citations styles are offered in this book.

The *MLA Handbook* uses parenthetical author-page citation. See pages 16-2 to 16-4 for examples of author-page citation.

The *APA Manual* uses parenthetical author-date citation See pages 17-2 to 17-5 for examples of author-date citation.

A Manual for Writers by Turabian uses endnotes or footnotes. Look at pages 18-2 to 18-3 for examples of endnote or footnote citation.

Each style has different rules for setting up margins, title pages, tables, illustrations, and quotations. Differences exist, too, in typing numbers, capitalization, and abbreviations. Carefully study your style's rules in Chapters 16, 17, or 18.

13.2. Write Your First Draft

1. Open a new document and save it as Research Paper Draft 1 or any title you choose.

2. Open your Outline file. Your Research Paper Draft 1 document and the Outline file will both be open.

3. Click on Window in the Tool bar. Click on View and Arrange All. Both files will be displayed horizontally as shown in Illustration 13.1. below.

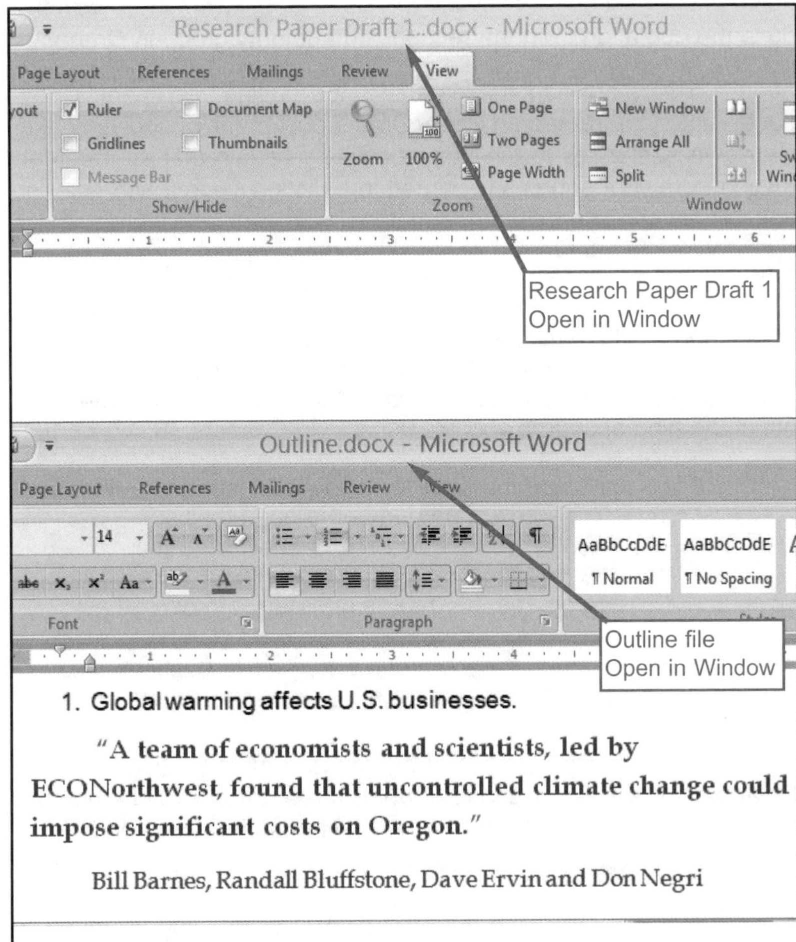

Illustration 13.1. Outline and Research Paper Draft 1

4. Scroll to the first topic sentence in your Outline Document. How does it sound? If you are comfortable with it, copy and paste it into your Research Paper Draft 1 document. Or you may want to write a sentence or two of your own to open the paragraph to enhance the topic sentence. Now look at the passages, quotes, paraphrases, or summaries under the first topic sentence in your Outline Document. Plan to use them as explanations, examples, contrasts, comparisons, illustrations, and statistical or authority statements.

In Illustration 13.2. on the next page, we have written our own sentence after the topic sentence beginning with "Although some business leaders deny the effects of global warming..." to introduce the quotation from the recognized authority group in Oregon.

5. Now highlight the material in the Outline Document. Copy-paste it into your Research Paper Draft 1 document immediately after your own sentences if any. Be absolutely certain that all the information from your sources is printed in a distinctive font and color so you will not confuse the source material with your own words. If it is a quotation, be sure to enclose it in quotation marks.

6. Next you must cite the source accurately in the text in the correct form. The minimum bibliographic information needed for the citation should be in the Outline file, but you should refer to its corresponding Bibliography file for detailed information. Find the sample of the type of source you are using in in Chapers 16, 17, or 18.

If you are using the MLA style you will insert the author's name and page number in parenthesis.

If you are using the APA style you will insert the author's name and the date of publication in parenthesis.

If you are using Turabian you will insert full bibliographic information in an endnote or footnote.

Note the correct MLA author-page citation for a Web site in Illustration 13.2. For citations of up to three authors, all names are listed. For more than three use the author's last name and et. al. See 16-2.

7. If you are using the MLA or APA styles, you will need to practice inserting the parenthetical citations in the text. The samples of parenthetical citations in Chapters 16 and 17 illustrate how to weave the citations into your text so the language flows.

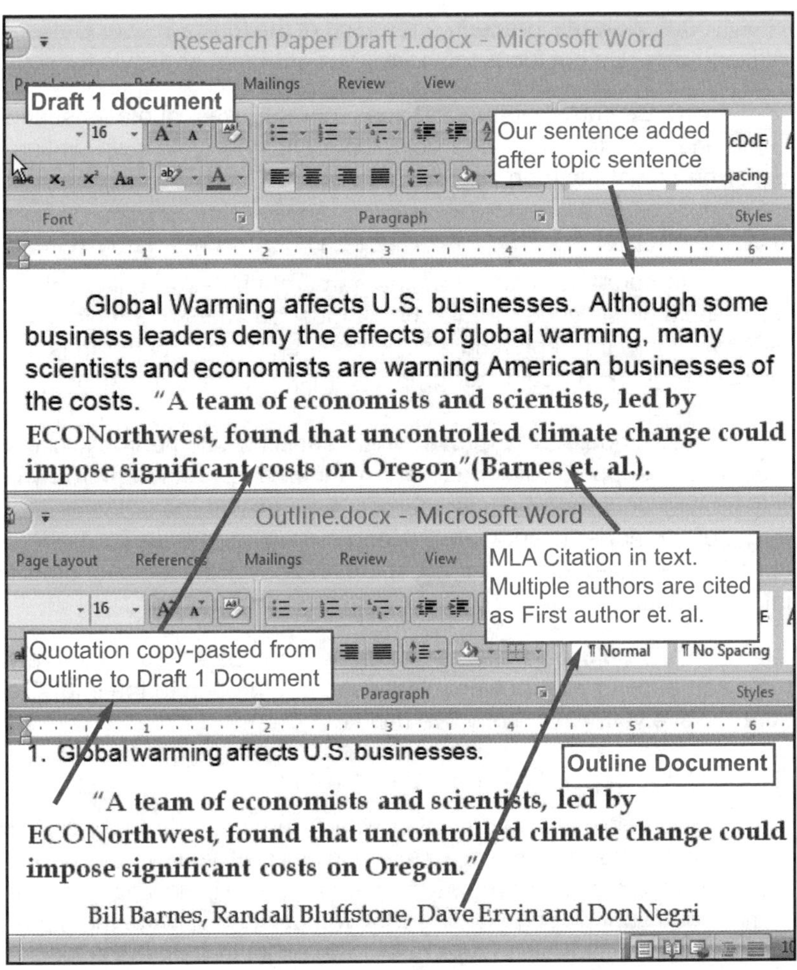

Illustration 13.2. Quote From Outline Into Draft 1

8. Continue the process building a coherent, unified, logically developed paragraph until all the appropriate supporting data for the first topic sentence is in your Research Paper Document Draft 1.

Smooth out the language adding appropriate transitions. Add your own sentences as necessary to produce fluent, clear writing and to serve as bridges and transitions to the supporting sentences. Do a quick check. Do your supporting sentences truly support and "prove" the topic sentence? Does your first paragraph have unity and coherence? Is it logically developed? Are parenthetical citations woven smoothly into the text?

9. Follow this procedure for each of the topics in your Outline. Write quickly. Do not focus too heavily on grammar and style for now.

10. Be sure that the passages, paraphrases, quotations, and summaries are in a font and color different from your own writing. Every one must have an appropriate citation.

13.3. Build Unity, Coherence, and Logic

Be sure your paper has the same attributes of unity, coherence and logic as your paragraphs. It must be about one major idea or thesis, the paragraphs must stick together, and the paper must be logically organized. Join paragraphs with appropriate transitions.

Your goal is to prove your Thesis Statement by using research to support your ideas and your writing. Although you will rely heavily on your research sources, be sure the major thesis and thrust of the paper is your own. Keep repeating, "I believe..." about your Thesis Statement. Do not just cut and paste the ideas of others into your paper.

Proceed until you have written powerful paragraphs for every topic sentence in your outline. Work straight through to the end. Be sure to save your work every five minutes.

13.4. Write The Introduction

It is better to wait until after writing the first draft to write your introduction. You will have a clearer picture of your whole paper. When you are ready, get your audience interested in delving into your work. You might begin by telling why you decided to write the paper or open with an interesting anecdote. You might include the positions others have taken on the subject. State your thesis and tell how you approached the subject. You could mention the major points in the paper or the reasons why your readers should be interested in the topic.

13.5. Write the Conclusion

Save writing the conclusion until after the first draft is done. Restate your thesis. Summarize the ideas and arguments you presented. Explain your conclusions. Discuss leads to further investigation. Tell why you think the topic is important, interesting and worthwhile. Congratulations! You have written your first draft! Print it and put it aside for a day. You will review it with clearer eyes when you are ready for the second draft.

Task 14

Write The Second Draft

Task 14: Write The Second Draft

Time for Task 13: 2 Hours

Your primary objective in writing your first draft was to prove your Thesis Statement by building your case paragraph by paragraph. Now your mind is clearer and you can be more objective about your writing. It is time to do some polishing of the project.

You are going to read your first draft now to improve its unity, coherence and logical organization.

14.1. Save Draft 1 as Draft 2.

Be sure you have saved the first draft. Open Draft 1 and save it as Research Paper Draft 2. You will have Draft 1 in case you lose Draft 2 inadvertently.

14.2. Proofread For Unity

Check: Clearly stated thesis in opening paragraph or paragraphs.
Action: Rewrite opening paragraphs if necessary.

Check: Each paragraph has a clear topic sentence and is about one idea.
Action: Rewrite weak paragraphs.

Check: Every paragraph supports thesis.
Action: Delete or rewrite extraneous paragraphs.

14.3. Proofread For Coherence

Check: All paragraphs stick together to support thesis.
Action: Move paragraphs for stronger coherence if necessary.

Check: Good transitional words and phrases join paragraphs.
Action: Rewrite transitional words and phrases.

14.4. Proofread For Logical Development

Check: Paragraphs intended to serve as explanations, examples, contrasts, comparisons, illustrations, statistics, and authority statements are arranged effectively to support your Thesis Statement.
Action: Move paragraphs to more effective locations.

14.5. Proofread for Proper Citations

Check: Bibliography file data matches citations.
Action: Eyeball every Bibliography file and citation. Make corrections.

Check: Citation format matches samples.
Action: Compare every citation entry against samples in Chapter 16, 17, or 18. Correct punctuation, italics, and format.

14.6. Proofread For Plagiarism

Check: Every source in distinctive font.
Action: Change fonts of any material needed.

Check: Quotation marks enclose quoted material
Action: Add quotation marks if necessary.

Check: Paraphrases and summaries do not include words, phrases, or similar sentence structure of original.
Action: Rewrite any questionable paraphrases or summaries.

Check: All source material is cited.
Action: Eyeball all source material and add citations if needed.

14.7. Use Content Checklist

When you are satisfied that Draft 2 has been thoroughly proofread and is more unified, coherent, and logically developed, use the Content Checklist on page 14-4 to be certain your paper meets the highest standards.

14.8. Print Draft 2

Print Research Paper Draft 2. Let it "cool off" overnight. When you feel ready, re-read it to see if the changes you made have improved the paper. Perhaps you may want to have a good friend or even your instructor critique it for you.

CONTENT CHECKLIST

- Thesis is clearly stated
- Paper is coherent
- Paper is unified
- Paper is logically developed
- Sources are properly cited
- Paper is checked for plagiarism
- Thesis is proved

Your paper is shaping up nicely. You feel confident that your thesis is clearly stated and every paragraph you wrote supports and helps to prove your thesis. You developed your paper in a logical fashion with paragraphs of example, illustration, explanation, authority statements, and statistics forming a sound foundation.

Good work! Go on to Task 15. Write The Final Draft in which you will further refine your writing with attention to spelling, grammar, usage, writing style, and possible bias.

Task 15

Write The Final Draft

Task 15: Write the Final Draft

Time for Task 15: 3 Hours

You wrote Research Paper Draft 2 to improve the content of your paper with particular attention to unity, coherence, and logical development. You also carefully checked your citations and made sure there was no inadvertent plagiarism. You are confident that you have proved your Thesis Statement with powerful arguments.

Now you want to be sure that your writing is free of grammatical and spelling errors and that your writing style is interesting and engaging. You also want to eliminate any sex, racial, ethnic, or other bias.

15.1. Save Draft 2 as Final Draft

Open Draft 2 and save it as Research Paper Final Draft. You will have Draft 1 in its original form, Draft 2 with your revisions, and a new document, Research Paper Final Draft. You will have Drafts 1 and 2 in case you lose the Final Draft inadvertently. Many instructors insist on seeing these drafts to show the progress of your work.

15.2. Change The Font and Color Of Sources

Now that you are certain all of your sources have been carefully cited you can change the fonts and colors of the pasted sources to the font and black of your own writing. Spacing may change when you change fonts so check to be sure everything is properly aligned.

15.3. Format Pages and Add Page Numbers

Prepare the appropriate heading, margins and pagination as shown in Chapters 16, 17, or 18. Each of the three styles format pages and place page numbers in different locations on the pages. Instructions are in Chapters 16, 17, and 18.

The MLA uses your name and the page number flush right and a half inch down from the top.

The APA uses an abbreviation of the title of your paper and the page number flush right and a half inch down from the top.

Turabian places numbers centered at the foot, at the top, or flush right at the top. Your instructor may specify the location.

15.4. Add Your Works Cited List, Bibliography, or References List

As you searched, you added each new source to your Bibliography file in proper alphabetical order. Delete any sources that you did not use in your paper. Check each bibliography entry against the samples in Chapters 16, 17, or 18. Be scrupulous about this task. Delete library call numbers and other locational information. Be sure all commas, periods, quotation marks, and italicized words are in the proper places.

15.5. Add Your Heading or Title Page

Prepare your heading or title page in appropriate MLA, APA, or Turabian style. Follow the samples in Chapters 16, 17, or 18.

15.6. Proofread for Spelling Errors.

Click on the Review tab and Spelling and Grammar in Microsoft Word. Microsoft will underline any misspelled word or even correct it as you type. If a word is misspelled, Word will offer you a dialog box with proposed changes. Find the correct one and click on Change.

Spell checkers are not perfect. Any unusual words not in their dictionaries as well as some common words will be missed. Spell checkers may not recognize misspellings when words are not in appropriate context. For example, see the sentence below:

> National preparedness for hurricanes in the ***year*** 2004 and 2005 was inadequate.

As you an see, ***year*** should be the plural, ***years***. Spell check would miss this error because **year** is not misspelled. Therefore, proofread very carefully. Use a late edition collegiate dictionary or Internet dictionary to check doubtful spellings.

15.7. Proofread For Grammatical Errors.

Click on the Review tab in Microsoft Word and Spelling & Grammar. Any ungrammatical words or phrases will be marked with a colored underline. A dialog box will open with the incorrect word or phrase underlined in the sentence with a proposed correction. Select the correction and Grammar Check will change it in your text.

As with Spell Check, the word processor's grammar checker may not catch all the errors. Review Part 3 of this book to find all the possible solecisms you may have committed in your writing. Pay particular attention to punctuation, agreement of subject and verb, agreement of pronouns and antecedents, proper use of pronouns, subordinate conjunctions, misplaced modifiers, and parallel construction.

15.8. Proofread For Best Writing Style

Check to be sure that you have varied your sentence openings with single word modifiers, prepositional phrases, participial phrases, and subordinate clauses. Have you varied sentence lengths using simple, compound, and complex sentences? Carefully check to be sure that you have been consistent in maintaining the same tense throughout the paper. Make appropriate revisions to improve writing style.

15.9. Proofread For Wordiness

Good writing is terse and sharp with no unnecessary words or phrases taking up space. Wordiness is the curse of all writers. As writers strive to get their words on paper, they sometimes mindlessly add superficial words that devalue the language. Some writers pad to reach the number of pages required for academic papers resulting in a wordy paper rife with unprecise language. Don't even think about padding. Becoming aware of the problem is the first step toward eliminating it. Read your paper with pages 12-9 to 12-11 of this book open to the ways you can get rid of any wordiness and sharpen your writing.

15.10. Proofread To Eliminate Jargon, Cliches, or Slang Language

Jargon, slang, and cliches do not belong in a scholarly research paper.

Words used primarily by insiders of a particular trade or profession that might not be easily understood by your readers are considered jargon. Words in law enforcement such as "perp" to mean perpetrator is an example. Eliminate terms that might not be understood and change them to standard English vocabulary.

Informal, non-standard words such as "bad" to mean very good or "punk" to mean a young male with bad character are examples of slang. Delete and replace slang terms with standard English.

Common expressions frequently heard in conversation such as "pitch black" to describe a dark night or "blazing hot" to describe a very warm day are examples of overused cliches. Become sensitized to the colloquialisms and cliches of common speech. Replace them with more sophisticated, standard English language.

15.11. Proofread For Sex, Racial, Ethnic, Religious, or Other Bias

Become sensitive to language that may be offensive or hurtful to others. Careful writers avoid language that may improperly generalize about gender, ethnic groups, socioeconomic class, sexual orientation, religion, and age. People decide for themselves how they wish to be named. Such decisions change over time. Be certain you are using the most appropriate appelation.

It is best to be as specific as possible. For example, saying someone is Asian casts them among an enormous group of many varied cultures. It is better to identify the specific country of origin as in Joan Kim is a Korean-American. Be careful when identifying groups or individuals to avoid implying one group's superiority over another's. For example, non-white suggests an unintended comparison. Avoid sexist gender definitions. Woman aviator implies that being a pilot is somehow unusual for a female. The chart below offers suggestions for appropriate language.

Improper Term	Better Term
mankind	people, humankind
stewardess	flight attendant
police woman	police officer
crippled	orthopedic disablilty
non-white, Oriental	African-American, Chinese
male nurse	nurse
chairman	chair, chairperson
salesmanship	sales ability
police woman	police officer
housewife	homemaker

15.12. How Does My Paper Stack Up

Let's do a final check:

1. Is your Thesis Statement clear? Do your readers know what you are trying to prove.
2. Are all the paragraphs arranged to positively support and prove your Thesis Statement?
3. Are all the paragraphs headed by topic sentences, unified and coherent?
4. Is your paper free of grammatical and spelling errors, jargon and cliches? Is your writing style varied? Is your writing sharp and clear and free of wordiness?
5. Are all your citations accurate and in correct form?
6. Is your bibliography accurate and in correct form?
7. Is your introduction interesting and motivating?
8. Does your conclusion tie it all up? Can your readers tell that you have proved your Thesis Statement.
9. Finally, have you formatted your paper properly?

If all checks out, you can submit your paper with a sense of pride and confidence that you have done your best. We hope it will earn you an A+.

CONGRATULATIONS: JOB WELL DONE!

Congratulations on the completion of your research paper! You, no doubt, have learned much about your thesis and you have sharpened your thinking, research, and writing skills. To be sure, you will use your newly honed skills to advantage in other pursuits in school, career, or other personal endeavors! Good luck!

Part 2

Using Research Writing Style Books

MLA Handbook
7th Edition, 2009

APA Manual
6th Edition, 2009

A Manual For Writers
7th Edition, 2007

MLA Handbook 7th Ed. 2009

PARENTHETICAL AUTHOR-PAGE CITATION IN THE TEXT

The author's name and the page number(s) of each source are placed in parenthesis in the text. When the author's name appears in the text only the page number(s) are placed in the parenthesis. A little practice may be necessary to insert the references and keep the writing fluent.

PUNCTUATION OF AUTHOR-PAGE CITATIONS

It is preferable to place the parenthetical reference at the end of the sentence. End the sentence without punctuation. Leave one space and add the parenthetical reference followed by the appropriate punctuation mark. Exception: When long quotations are set off from the text, leave one space after the end punctuation and add the parenthetical reference without any punctuation.

WORKS CITED LIST

Every source cited in the text must be documented in the Works Cited list at the end of the paper.

MLA AUTHOR-PAGE CITATION SAMPLES

WORK - SINGLE AUTHOR

Insert the last name(s) of the author(s) and page number(s) in the parentheses. If two authors have same last name, add the first initial.

This concept has been reported earlier (Jones 148).

or

If author's name appears in the text, insert only the page number(s) in the parenthesis.

Jones reported this concept (148).

WORK- MULTIPLE AUTHORS

Insert all authors' last names and the page number(s) in the parenthesis. If more than 3 authors insert first author and et. al.

An opposing idea has been explored (Brown, Smith, and Rogers 179-81).

or

If authors' names appear in the text, insert only the page number(s) in the parenthesis.

Brown, Smith, and Rogers explored a new idea (179-81).

MULTIPLE WORKS BY THE SAME AUTHOR(S)

If two or more works by the same author(s) will be cited, insert author(s) name(s) followed by a comma, the title, if short or shorten, and the page number(s) in the parenthesis.

Most humans experience depression, often for reasons unknown to them (Rogers, *Psychology* 171-73).

or

If author(s) name(s) and title appear in the text, insert only the page number(s) in the parenthesis.

In *Psychology and Modern Man*, Rogers explains that most humans experience depression, often for reasons unknown to them (171-73).

or

If author's name appears in text, insert the title and page number in the parentheses. If author's name is in text, cite title and page number(s) in parentheses.

Rogers explains that most humans experience depression, often for reasons unknown to them (*Psychology and Modern Man* 171-173).

WHOLE WORK WITH NO PAGE NUMBERS

Include in text instead of parenthesis author, editor, performer who will be listed in Works Cited.

Weintraub's adapted his screenplay for the *Tekkonkinkreet* film from the original Japanese manga.

MULTI-VOLUME WORK

Insert author's name and volume number followed by a colon, space and page number(s) in parentheses.

Economic policy should provide for maintenance of full employment (Johnson 2: 273).

or

If author's name and volume appear in the text, place only the page number(s) in parentheses.

In volume 2, Johnson suggests that economic policy should provide for maintenance of full employment (273).

or

If the whole volume is cited without reference to pages, insert the author's name and abbreviation for volume in the parentheses.

Economic policy should provide for maintenance of full employment (Johnson, vol. 2).

CORPORATE OR GOVERNMENT PUBLICATIONS

Insert corporate author in text and place page number(s) in parentheses. Best to use long names in text to avoid long parenthetical citation. Use abbreviations when possible in parenthesis.

In 1984 the United States Department of Defense issued a report denying activity in Paraguay (31).

or

Insert corporate author and page number(s) in parentheses.

A recent report denies any United States activity in Paraguay (U.S. Dept. of Defense 31).

MAGAZINE, JOURNAL, AND ONLINE SOURCES

Use same techniques as for books

NOVELS

Insert the page number followed by a semicolon and the chapter number preceded by the abbreviation for the part or chapter.

The opening words of *Moby Dick*, “Call me Ishmael,” quickly identify the narrator (1; ch.1).

PLAYS

Insert division: act, scene, canto, book, or part and line(s) separated by periods in the parentheses but omit page numbers. In general, use arabic numerals rather than roman unless otherwise directed.

The queen finds relief in believing her son, Hamlet, mad (3.4.105).

POETRY

Cite by division and line: canto, book, or part separated by periods in the parenthesis (similar to plays), but omit page numbers. If only lines are cited, spell out the word, line or lines, and type the number(s).

Shelley's "Ozymandias" ironically describes the ephemeral nature of fame and power in the statement, "Look on my works, ye Mighty, and despair! / Nothing beside remains (lines 10-13).

WORKS LISTED BY TITLE

Insert title or abbreviation and page number(s) in parentheses unless the title appears in the text.

The *New Yorker* reprinted a story on country dining (“Country Inns and Byways” 213).

or

Insert title of whole unsigned work in parentheses

The spectrum is visible when white light is sent through a prism (“Color and Light”).

or

The information appeared in *House of Cards.*

WORKS CITED

A bibliography called Works Cited, printed on a separate page at the end of the paper, provides complete publication information for all of the sources cited in your paper. The citations in the text must lead the reader to the corresponding sources in the Works Cited bibliography.

Start the list on a new page but continue the pagination. Center the words, Works Cited, in upper and lower case one inch from the top. Double space and type the first entry. Type the first line flush left and indent following lines, if any, one half inch. Double space between and within entries. Entries are arranged in strict alphabetical order ignoring punctuation marks in names.

NONPERIODICAL PRINT PUBLICATIONS

SAMPLES SHOWN BELOW ARE SINGLE SPACED TO SAVE SPACE

BOOK - ONE AUTHOR

Author. *Title*. City: Publisher, Date. Print.

Gershman, Herbert S. *The Surrealist Revolution in France.* Ann Arbor: U of Michigan P, 2008. Print.

BOOK - MULTIPLE AUTHORS

List names in same order as on title page. Do not alphabetize. Cite only first author last name first.

Raffer, Bernard C., Richard Friedman, and Robert A. Baron. *New York in Financial Crisis.* New York: Harper, 2009. Print.

BOOK - CORPORATE AUTHOR

Author can be committee, commission, or association. Corporate author may also be publisher. Omit initial articles, A, The in name or author.

National Policy Association. *Welfare Reform*. New York: National Policy Assn., 2007. Print.

MLA WORKS CITED SAMPLES

BOOK - ANONYMOUS AUTHOR

***Title*. City: Publishers, Date.**

Handbook of Pre-Columbian Art. New York: Johnson, 2002. Print.

AN ANTHOLOGY OR COMPILATION

Name of editor or compiler, ed. or comp. *Title*. City: Publisher, Date.

Jones, Robert, ed. *New York by Night*. New York: Hyperion, 2009. Print.

WORK IN AN ANTHOLOGY

Author of work. "Title in quotation marks." . Ed. Trans. or Comp. for editor, translator, or compiler of work if any. Name. *Anthology Title*. Ed. Trans. Comp. of anthology. Name. Publication City: Publisher, Date. Page numbers. Print.

Pope, Alexander. "Solitude." *The Book of Living Verse.* Ed. Louis Untermeyer. New York: Harcourt, Brace and Company, 1945. 172-173. Print.

PREVIOUSLY PUBLISHED EDITED OR TRANSLATED WORK IN AN ANTHOLOGY

Author of work. *Title italicized.* Ed. or Trans. for editor or translator. Name. *Anthology Title*. Ed. Name. Publication City: Publisher: Date. Page numbers. Print.

Voltaire, Francois-Marie. *Candide*. Trans. Louis Marshall. *Great French Drama.* Ed. Vincent Roselli. New York: Rogers and Company, 1989. 89-117. Print.

ARTICLE IN WIDELY USED REFERENCE BOOK - UNSIGNED

List only the edition, if stated, and year of publication.

"Article Title." *Reference Book Title*. xx ed. Print.

"DNA." *Encyclopedia Americana*. 1994 ed. Print.

ARTICLE IN SPECIALIZED REFERENCE BOOK

Cite full bibliographic data.

Author. "Article Title." *Reference Work Title*. Ed. Editor's Name. 4th ed. Vol. 2. Publication City: Publisher, Date. Print.

Johnson, Roger P. "Family Values." *Encyclopedia of Social Work.* Ed. Larry Davis. 20th ed. Vol. 2. New York: Oxford University Press, 2009. Print.

MLA WORKS CITED SAMPLES

FOREWORD, PREFACE, INTRODUCTION

Author. Foreword, Preface, Introduction. *Title.* By Last name of author if same as author of part. Full name if author of work is different from part author. City: Publisher, Date. Page number(s). Print.

Burnisky, Thomas. Foreword. *The Third Avenue L.* By Jay Burnisky. New York: Fenton, 2001. v-vi. Print.

Coronista, Claire. Introduction. *Lives of World War II Generals.* By Shari Rogers. New York: Bantam, 1999. ii-iv. Print.

SCHOLARLY EDITION OF A WORK

Author. *Title.* Ed. Editor's name. City: Publisher, Date. Print.

Melville, Herman. *Moby Dick.* Ed. J.P. Small. Boston: Houghton, 1973. Print.

A TRANSLATION

Author. *Title.* Trans. Translator's name. City: Publisher, Date.

Flaubert, Gustave. *Madame Bovary*. Trans. Max Aveling. New York: Harper and Brothers, 1950. Print.

AN ILLUSTRATED BOOK OR GRAPHIC NOVEL

Give illustrator's name after title when illustrations are secondary to the text.

Author. *Title.* Illus. Illustrator's Name. City: Publisher, Date. Print.

Montgomery, M.R., Gerald L. Foster. *A Field Guide to Airplanes of North America.* Illus. Gerald L. Foster. New York: Houghton Mifflin, 1992. Print.

SECOND OR LATER EDITIONS

Enter edition number or revised edition after editor, translator, or compiler if any. If none, after title.

Cragstone, Marvin. *History of Afghanistan*. Rev. ed. New York: Jonsie Press, 2006. Print.

Smith, Carol. *Comic Books and the Psychological Development of Children.* Ed. George Cropis. 2nd ed. New York: Knopf, 2008. Print.

MLA WORKS CITED SAMPLES

MULTIVOLUME WORK - CITING MORE THAN ONE VOLUME

State total volumes after title or after any editor's name. Cite references to volume and page numbers in the text of your paper, not in Works Cited.

Smith, Richard K. *A History of Religion in the United States.* 4 vols. Chicago: U of Chicago, 2007. Print.

MULTIVOLUME WORK - CITING ONE VOLUME ONLY

State number of volume used and publication information for that volume only. Cite page numbers in the text of your paper.

Smith, Richard K. *A History of Religion in the United States*. Vol. 3. Chicago: U of Chicago, 2007. Print.

MULTIVOLUME WORK WITH AN INDIVIDUAL TITLE

OK to cite the work without citing other volume numbers

Churchill, Winston S. *Triumph and Tragedy.* Boston: Houghton Mifflin, 1953. Print.

MULTIVOLUME WORK EACH WITH INDIVIDUAL TITLES SUPPLEMENTARY INFORMATION

If desired, the additional information may be included. Add *of* and *Title of Entire Multivolume Work*

Churchill, Winston S. *Triumph and Tragedy*. Boston: Houghton Mifflin, 1953. Vol. 6 of *The Second World War.* 6 Vols. 1948-1953. Print.

BOOK IN A SERIES

Add the series name and number, if any, after the full listing.

Jonsone, Carol. *Learning and Teaching in America*. Ed. Richard Corwin. Berkeley: U of California P, 2008. Print. Education in America 6.

REPUBLISHED BOOK OR JOURNAL

Insert the original publication date before the bibliographic data for the later republished edition.

Frazier, Charles. *Cold Mountain*. 1997. New York: Vintage-Random, 1998. Print.

MLA WORKS CITED SAMPLES

PAMPHLET, BROCHURE, OR PRESS RELEASE

Cite same as a book.

Health Topics for Teenagers. Detroit: Anthem Press, 2002. Print.

GOVERNMENT AGENCY PUBLICATION

Government. Agency. *Title.* City: Publisher, Date.

United States. Dept. of Labor. *Labor Relations in the Steel Industry.* Washington: GPO, 2001. Print.

New York. Dept. of Correctional Services. *Fact Sheet: Prison Closure:* New York: 2003. Print.

TWO OR MORE WORKS FROM SAME GOVERNMENT OR AGENCY

For the second and later entries, replace the name of the government and/or the name of the agency with 3 hyphens each.

United States. Dept. of Labor. *Labor Relations in the Steel Industry.* Washington: GPO, 2001. Print.

---. ---. *Immigrant Employment Policies.* Washington: GPO, 2002.

U.S. Congressional Record

Cite only date, page numbers and medium.

Cong. Rec. 12 Jan. 2009: 4831-4833. Print.

PUBLISHED PROCEEDINGS OF A CONFERENCE

Cite like a book.

Charterson, Amy, Norbert Stone, and Peter Nochansky, ed. *Proceedings of the 2003 Annual Meeting of the Phillips Reading Consortium.* Cincinnati: Phillips Society, 2003. Print.

PUBLISHED PRESENTATION AT PROCEEDINGS OF A CONFERENCE

Cite like a work in a collection.

Greenberg, John. "Dyslexia and Brain Patterns." *Proceedings of the 2003 Annual Meeting of the Phillips Reading Consortium.* Cincinnati: Phillips Society, 2003. Print.

DISSERTATION - UNPUBLISHED

Author. "Title." Diss. Institution, Date.

Samson, Robert. "The Influence of Economic Deprivation on Academic Achievement." Diss. New York U, 1999. Print.

PERIODICAL PRINT PUBLICATIONS

ARTICLE IN A SCHOLARLY JOURNAL WITH CONTINUOUS PAGINATION

Author. "Article Title." *Journal Title* Volume Number. Issue Number (Date): Page numbers of complete article. Print. However, cite specific page numbers in your text.

Zirkel, Perry A. "School Law All Stars: Two Successive Constellations." *Phi Delta Kappan* 90.10 (June 2009): 704-708. Print.

ARTICLE IN A SCHOLARLY JOURNAL THAT USES ONLY ISSUE NUMBERS

Cite the issue numbers instead of Volume and Issue number

Aksoy, Ozan E. "The Politicization of Kurdish Folk Songs in Turkey in the 1990s." *Journal of Musical Anthropology of the Mediterranean* 11 (2006): 34-39. Print.

NEWSPAPER ARTICLE

Omit articles a, the, from newspaper names. Insert [city name of local papers] in brackets after newspaper name without punctuation. Abbreviate all months except May, June, July. State all page numbers of article in works cited, but cite exact page numbers in text.

Author. "Article Title." *Newspaper Name* Day Month Year, ed.: page number(s). Print.

Bennett, James. "Abbas in Clash Over His Stance in Peace Talks." *New York Times* 9 July 2003, late ed.: A1+. Print.

In a local paper

O'Dell, Rob. "City OKs Tax Hikes on Array of Services." *Arizona Daily Star* [Tucson] 10 June 2009, early ed.: A1+. Print.

MLA WORKS CITED SAMPLES

NEWSPAPER ARTICLE IN PAPERS THAT HAVE SECTIONS

Barron, James. "Clinics Closed By Overspending." *New York Times* 20 July 2003, late ed., sec. 1: 31+. Print.

MAGAZINE ARTICLE

Author. "Title." *Magazine Name* Date: page numbers. Print.
For weekly magazines cite day, month, year. For monthly or bi-monthly magazines cite month and year. If not on consecutive pages add a + after the page number.

Tanenhaus, Sam. "Bush's Brain Trust." *Vanity Fair* July 2003: 114+ Print.

Cooper, James C. "The Skittish Bond Market Won't Shake Housing For Now." *BusinessWeek* 14 July 2003: 29-30. Print.

A REVIEW

Reviewer's name. "Review Title if there is one." Rev. of *Title of Work Reviewed,* by Author's Name. *Name of Publication* Date: page numbers. Print. Abbreviate all months except May, June, and July. If an editor, translator, or director is being reviewed insert dir., trans., or ed., instead of by.

Als, Hilton. "Movers and Shakers." Rev. of Boogaloo: The Quintessence of American Popular Music, by Arthur Kempton. *New Yorker* 7 July 2003: 76-77. Print.

ABSTRACT IN AN ABSTRACTS JOURNAL

First cite the publication data for the original source. Follow with the data for the abstract journal. *Abstracts Journal Title* volume number. issue number, (year): item number or page number(s). Print.
Include word, item, before any item numbers. If title of journal does not include the word Abstracts, insert it followed by a period before the abstract journal title.

Frischman, Josephine K. "Analysis of Bias in Selecting Test Times." *Journal of Experimental Psychology* 98 (1992): 325-31. Psychological Abstracts 80 (1993): item 7321. Print.

Petersen, Sandra. "Issues in Affirmative Action." *Research in Higher Education* 34 (1993): 612-620. Abstract. *Current Index to Journals in Education* 26 (1994): item EK392018. Print.

MLA WORKS CITED SAMPLES

ANONYMOUS ARTICLE

"Article Title." *Title of Magazine* Day Month Year: Page number(s). Print.

"Witchcraft Trials Again." *Time* 17 May 2002: 35. Print.

UNSIGNED EDITORIAL

"Title." Editorial. *Publication Title* Day Month Year, ed.: Print.
Abbreviate all months except May, June, July.

"Big Food Gets the Obesity Message." Editorial. *New York Times* 10 July 2009, late ed.: A22. Print.

EDITORIAL - SIGNED

Author. "Title." Editorial. *Publication Title.* Day Month Year: page number. Print.
Abbreviate all months except May, June, July.

Hartmann, Joseph. "Ethical Decisions." Editorial. *Newsweek* 12 Jan. 2009: 23. Print.

LETTER TO THE EDITOR

Author. Letter. *Publication Title* Day Month Year, ed., sec.: page number. Print.

Christopher, Catinberg. Letter. *New York Times* 11 July 2003, late ed., sec. 2: 3. Print.

NONPERIODICAL WEB PUBLICATIONS

WEB SITES INCLUDING NEWSPAPERS AND MAGAZINES CITED ONLY ON THE WEB

It is difficult to determine various parts of Web sites. Use your best judgement to identify the parts described below. If there is no title, use Home page or Online posting in place of title. Periods follow all parts except the publisher or sponsor.

It is best to try to reach the site again by using your citation. If not successful, try other arrangements of Web site title, author and article titles until you can retrieve the same site. Include URLs only when you cannot return to the Web site with your citation.

MLA WORKS CITED SAMPLES

Include the following:
Name of author, editor, performer or translator if any. *Title of Work* or "Title if part of larger work." *Title of Web site.* nth ed. if any. Publisher or sponsor or N.p. if not avail able, Day Month Year of Publication or n.d. if not avail able. Web. Access Date Day Month Year.

"Administration To Issue New Wall Street Pay Curbs." *National Public Radio.* Natl. Public Radio, 10 June 2009. Web. 20 August 2009.

Alter, Jonathan. "Peanut Butter Politics." *Newsweek*. Newsweek, 12 June 2009. Web. 4 Sept. 2009.

WEB SITES THAT ALSO APPEARED IN PRINT

Include the bibliographic data for the publication following the formats for nonperiodical print sources. Follow with the *Title of Web site*. Web. Day Month Year of access.

Stutely, Richard. *Guide to Economic Indicators: Making Sense of Economics.* 5th ed. New York: Bloomberg Press, 2003. *Google Book Search.* Web. 22 Aug. 2009.

United States. Dept. of Education. Institute of Educational Sciences. *Reading Recovery*. 2007. *What Works Clearing House. Web. 8 Sept. 2009.*

WEB SITES THAT ALSO APPEARED IN NON-PRINT MEDIA SUCH AS FILM, SOUND RECORDING, OR WORK OF ART

To cite a Web site that contains a reproduction of a film or sound recording, first enter the bibliographic data for the work in its original form. See pages 16-15. Then add the *Web site Title*. Web. Day Month Year of access. Abbreviate all months except May, June, July.

Picasso, Pablo. *The Barefoot Girl.* 1895. Musée Picasso, Paris. *Olga's Gallery.* Web. 7 May 2009.

SCHOLARLY JOURNAL INCLUDING ARTICLES, REVIEWS, ETC. ONLY ON THE WEB

First cite the publication as in Periodical Print Publications. See page 16-10 to 16-12. Web journals may not include page numbers. If so, use n. pag. Or they may have page numbers in different sequence. Then add Web. and Day, Month, Year of access. Abbreviate all months except May, June, July.

Potter, Emily. "Climate Change and the Problem of Representation." *Australian Humanities Review* 46 (2009): 69-77. Web. 12 Aug. 2009.

PERIODICAL PUBLICATION IN ONLINE DATABASE

Databases offer pdf and html files of articles that may differ from the original articles previously in print. These articles may have hypertext links to other sources and other material not found in print. Web journals may not include page numbers. If so, use n. pag. Or they may have page numbers in different sequence. First cite the publication as in Periodical Print Publications. See page 16-10 to 16-12. Then add *Database Title*. Web. Day Month, Year of access. Abbreviate all months except May, June, July.

Coghill. J. "Herman Melville: An Introduction." *Choice* 46.3 (2008): n. pag. *Platinum Periodicals*. Web. 7 Aug. 2009.

OTHER COMMON SOURCES

TELEVISION OR RADIO BROADCAST

"Episode Title." Program Title. Network Name if available. Call letters, City. Broadcast date. Medium, Additional data.

"Pollution in the Desert." *Sixty Minutes*. CBS. WCBS, New York. 6 Mar. 1994. Television.

Include information on directors, writers, narrators, etc. after episode or after program which ever is appropriate.

"Obama Pushes Congress To Work On Health Care" Narr. Mara Liasson. *Morning Edition*. Natl. Public Radio. WNYC, New York, 8 June 2009. Radio

"Obama Pushes Congress To Work On Health Care" *Morning Edition*. Dir. John Schwartz. Natl. Public Radio. WNYC, New York, 8 June 2009. Radio

MLA WORKS CITED SAMPLES

MUSICAL SOUND RECORDING

Cite first whoever is emphasized: Composer. Performer. Conductor. *Title*. Perf. Other Artists. Manufacturer, Year of Issue or if unknown, n.d. Audiocassette, Audiotape, CD, or LP.

If citing a specific song, place quotation marks around it.

Webber, Andrew Lloyd. *Phantom of the Opera*. Perf. Michael Crawford, Sarah Brightman, and Steve Barton. EMI, 1987. Audiocassette.

SPOKEN SOUND RECORDING

Speaker or Director, narr. *Title of Work read.* By Author of Work. Manufacturer, Year of Issue or if unknown, n.d. Audiocassette, Audiotape, CD, or LP.

Thomas, Richard, narr. *Team of Rivals.* By Doris Kearns Goodwin. Simon & Schuster, 2005. Audiocassette.

FILM OR VIDEO RECORDING

TITLE. Director. Also if pertinent, Writers, Performers, Producers, Distributor, Year.

WALL-E. Dir. Frank Stanton. Walt Disney Pictures, 2008. Film.

Or begin with name of special person associated with film. Abbreviations of special person titles are lower case. dir. perf. adapt.

Spielberg, Steven, dir. *Raiders of the Lost Ark.* Perf. Harrison Ford. Paramount, 1982. Film.

PLAY - DANCE - OPERA - CONCERT

***Title*. By Author. Prominent persons associated with performance such as Directors, Performers, Conductors. Name of Theater, City. Performance Date. Performance.**

The Importance of Being Earnest. By Oscar Wilde. Dir. Robert Richmond. Baruch Performing Arts Center, New York. 12 July 2003. Performance.

Begin with name of special person associated with performance

Pavarotti, Luciano, perf. *Tosca* By Giacomo Puccini. With Carol Vaness and Samuel Ramey. Metropolitan Opera. Cond. James Levine. Metropolitan Opera House, New York. 10 March 2004. Performance.

MLA WORKS CITED SAMPLES

SCORE OR LIBRETTO OF MUSICAL COMPOSITION

Treat same as a book.

Composer's name. *Title of composition, form, number and key* as it appears on title page. Capitalize No. and Op. Date of Composition or if unknown, N.d. Place of Publication: Publisher's Name, Date of Publication. Medium.

Tchaikovsky, Piotr Ilyich. *Violin Concerto in D major*, Op. 35. 1878. New York: Mutopia, 2004. Print.

PHOTOGRAPHS - PAINTINGS - SCULPTURES

Artist's name. *Work Title.* Date of Composition. If unavailable write N.d. Medium. Museum or location of work. City.

If collector unknown, use Private collection instead of museum.

Mount, William Sidney. *Cider Making*. 1841. Oil. Metropolitan Museum of Art, New York.

INTERVIEW - BROADCAST

Interviewee. Interview by interviewer. *Program Name*. Station, City. Date. Medium.

If interview is part of a series or program, enclose title in quotation marks.

Giuliani, Rudolph. Interview by Charlie Rose. *Charlie Rose*. WNET, New York. 6 May 2003. Television.

INTERVIEWS - PERSONAL

Interviewee. Interview Type. Date.

Wiesel, Elie. Personal Interview. 11 Jan. 2006.

Chambers, Brad. Telephone interview. 11 Dec.2008.

MAP OR CHART

***Name of map or chart.* Chart or Map. Publisher, Date. Print.**

Kenya. Map. New York: Hagstroms, 2001. Print.

Airspace Designations. Chart. Englewood, CO: Jeppesen-Sanderson, 2009. Print.

MLA WORKS CITED SAMPLES

CARTOON OR COMIC STRIP

Artist's name. "Title if any." Cartoon or Comic strip. *Publication* Day Month Year of Publication: Abbreviate all except May, June, July. Page Number. Print.

Smaller, Barbara. Cartoon. *New Yorker* 7 July 2003: 40. Print.

Millar, Jeff, and Bill Hinds. "Tank McNamara." Comic strip. *Washington Post* 3 Mar. 2002: 26. Print.

ADVERTISEMENT

Company or product. Advertisement. *Name of publication or medium* Date: Page if print medium. Print.

Tiffany. Advertisement. *New York Times* 10 July 2009, late ed.: A3. Print.

SPEECH - ADDRESS - READING - LECTURE

Speaker's name. "Title if any." Meeting name if any. Sponsoring Organization. Meeting Place, City. Day Month Year. Lecture, Keynote Speech, Address or Reading.

Lewis, Bernard. "Jihad and Contemporary Politics." Lectures and Conversations. 92nd Street Y, New York. 22 Dec. 2003. Lecture.

TYPESCRIPT OR MANUSCRIPT

Author. *Title or Material Description* or in "Quotation Marks if an article, essay, story or poem in a larger work." Composition Date or N.d. if not known. MS for hand written or TS for typescript Name of Holder, Location City.

Melville, Herman. *Typee*. 1846. MS Arrowhead, Pittsfield.

LETTER - MEMO - E-MAIL - TEXT MESSAGE

Cite same as a work in a collection. Add date of letter and any Letter writer's name. "Title of Letter." Day Month Year of writing. Letter number if any of *Title of Collection.* Ed. or Trans. if any. Name of Editor or Translator. Publication City: Publisher, Date. Page numbers. Print.

MLA WORKS CITED SAMPLES

LETTER - MEMO - E-MAIL - TEXT MESSAGE

Lincoln, Abraham. "To Mrs. Bixby." 21 Nov. 1864. *Collected Works of Abraham Lincoln.* Ed. Roy P. Basler. Springfield: Abraham Lincoln Association, 2006. Print.

Bricson, Robert. "Warning re: Market Meltdown." Message to John Cohen. 6 Aug. 2009. E-mail.

Caruthers, Jonathan. "Budget Projections for Lawrence Schools." Message to Joan Smarther. 4 Apr. 2009. Text Message.

UNPUBLISHED LETTER

Cite same as a manuscript.

Letter writer's name. Letter to name. Day Month Year. MS. Title of Collection, City.

Churchill, Winston. Letter to Franklin Delano Roosevelt. 18 July 1942. MS. Churchill Society. London.

ARTICLE IN MICROFORM COLLECTION

Newsbank and other services publish articles on microforms.

Begin with original publication information for an article or other source. Microfiche or microform. *Title of microform source* Volume number (Year): identifying numbers fiche 2, grids 6-9.

Chieper, Randy. "Welfare Reform Debates." *New York Times* 20 Apr. 1994, late ed.: A12. Microform. *Newsbank: Welfare and Social Problems* 17 (1994): fiche 2, grids A9-13.

ARTICLE IN LOOSELEAF COLLECTION
SOCIAL ISSUES RESOURCES SERIES - SIRS

Social Issues Resources Series (SIRS) and other services publish articles on special topics in loose-leaf books.

Begin with original publication information for an article or other source. Print. Add *Looseleaf Information.* Ed. if any. Vol. #. Publication City: Publisher, Publication year. Article number abbreviated Art.

ARTICLE IN LOOSELEAF COLLECTION
SOCIAL ISSUES RESOURCES SERIES - SIRS

Johnson, Roger K. "Aircraft Crashes Due To Icing." *Aviation News* June 2009: 31+. Print. *Aviation Safety*. Ed. Josh Droney. Vol. 3. Boca Raton: SIRS, 2009. Art. 31.

PUBLICATION ON CD-ROM OR DVD-ROM

Suppliers and Vendors: Always distinguish between the supplier of information and publishers. Sometimes they are the same. Some providers lease to several vendors. You must cite the vendor's name in the works-cited list.

Publication dates: Because some published databases are updated annually or quarterly, you must cite the publication date of the document as well as the publication date of the database in the works-cited list.

NONPERIODICAL PUBLICATION ON CD-ROM OR DVD-ROM

Cite same as a book.

Author. *Title*. Ed. Editor's name. Edition, release, or version if any. Publication City: Publisher, Date. CD-ROM or DVD-ROM.

Melville, Herman. *Moby Dick.* Ed. J.P. Small. Boston: Houghton, 1973. CD-ROM.

PERIODICAL PUBLICATION ON CD-ROM OR DVD-ROM

Journals, magazines, newspapers, abstract collections, and bibliographies on CD-ROM and DVD-ROM

Begin with bibliographic information for the print source.

Author's name if any. "Article Title." *Publication Title*. Publication Date: Page number(s). CD-ROM or DVD-ROM. *Database Title*. Vendor. Database publication date.

Krensis, Colette. "AIDS Education Programs." *AIDS in America* Mar. 2008: 32+ Abstract. CD-ROM. Periodical Abstracts Ondisc. UMI-ProQuest. June 2008.

DIGITAL FILE

Digital files are those that are not on the Web or a CD or DVD. They might be a Microsoft Word file, a PDF file, a JPEG file, MP3 file, XML file.

Cite as you would for a recording, a book, a photograph using the samples in these pages. Instead of the medium names: Print, Web, or CD-ROM, cite the type of digital format plus the word, file . If you do not know the file type, state Digital file.

American Memory. "Prosperity and Thrift: The Coolidge Era." 1929. Lib. of Cong., Washington. JPEG file.

Sandler, Adam, perf. "Somebody Kill Me." *The Wedding Singer: Music from the Motion Picture,* Sony BMG, 1998. MP3 file.

PROSE

SHORT QUOTATIONS

Quotations of four lines or less are not set off from the text but are placed within double quotation marks. Quotations may be placed at the beginning, middle, or end of sentences. Insert short phrases and words directly into the sentence enclosed in double quotation marks.

Thomas Paine, in his pamphlet, The Crisis, wrote the stirring line, "These are the times that try men's souls."

If the quotation ends the sentence and a parenthetical citation is required, omit the period in the sentence and place the period after the reference citation.

Thomas Paine, in his pamphlet, The Crisis, wrote the stirring line, "These are the times that try men's souls" (14).

LONG QUOTATIONS

For longer quotations, use a comma or colon after the last word of text, double space and type the quotation with no quotation marks. Indent one inch from the left margin and double space quote. Place the the citation after the sentence punctuation in quotations set off from the text.

Writing to bolster the country after the discouraging first days of the war, Paine wrote:

> These are the times that try men's souls. The summer soldier and the sunshine patriot will, in this crisis, shrink from the service of their country; but he that stands it now, deserves the love and thanks of man and woman. (18)

If two or more paragraphs are quoted one after another, indent the first line of each paragraph three more spaces or an additional quarter of an inch. If the first sentence quoted does not begin a paragraph in the original, do not indent it. Copy any quotation marks within the original quotation. Use double quotation marks for quotations within a long quotation. Place the the citation after the sentence punctuation in quotations set off from the text.

In *Master and Commander* Captain Jack Aubrey has his mate, Mr. Mowett, explain the nomenclature of early 19th century sailing ships to his good friend, Dr. Maturin, to help his readers gain the same understanding:

> 'And that's the mainstays'l they just set, below us. And that's the forestays'l for'ard: you never see one, but on a man-of-war.'
>
> 'Those triangles? Why are they called staysails?' asked Stephen, speaking at random. (4)

SHORT POETRY

Poetry of three lines or fewer is placed in double quotation marks within the text. Separate lines of poetry which appear in a single line of text by a slash (/) with a space before and after the slash. When a quotation ends a line place the period after the citation.

Robert Frost's short poem tells how man is challenged by the unknown, ends with the lines, "Two roads diverged in a wood, and I / I took the one less traveled by, / And that has made all the difference (11).

LONGER POETRY

For poetry more than three lines long begin on a new line and indent each line one inch from the left margin. Double space. Do not add quotation marks unless they occur in the original poetry. Reproduce the original format of unusual poetry if possible. Lines which do not fit on one line should be continued on the next line and indented an additional quarter inch. To improve appearance, it is OK to indent less than one inch if that will allow the longer lines to fit on one text line. Unusually spaced poetry should be followed as closely as possible. Place the the citation after the sentence punctuation in quotations set off from the text.

O'Shaughnessy's "Ode" captures the spirit of human creativity:

We are the music makers,

  And we are the dreamers of dreams,

Wandering by lone sea-breakers,

  And sitting by desolate streams-

World-losers and world forsakers,

  On whom the pale moon gleams-

Yet we are the movers and shakers

  Of the world forever, it seems. (6)

DRAMA

Use a comma or colon after the last word of text, double space one inch from the left margin. Type the character's name in all caps, punctuate with a period and type the quotation. Indent following lines by the same character an additional one quarter inch. Begin following character's lines by indenting one inch. Stage directions are quoted exactly as in the original text. Parenthetical citations follow the punctuation at the end of the last quoted line.

The opening lines of Shakespeare's Hamlet create a mood of foreboding with this exchange between the guards:

MARCELLUS. What! has this thing appear'd again tonight?

BERNARDO. I have seen nothing.

MARCELLUS. Horatio says 'tis but our fantasy,

And will not let belief take hold of him

Touching this dreaded sight twice seen of us: (1.1.21-26)

PUNCTUATION OF QUOTATIONS

Begin quotations with a comma or no punctuation if the quotation is part of the non-quoted sentence.

Einstein claimed that "The theory of relativity can be outlined in a few words" (131).

MLA QUOTATIONS

Begin a quotation with a colon if it is a separate sentence.

Einstein ended his pacifist stance with these words: "The time seems inauspicious for further advocacy of certain propositions of the radical pacifist movement." (414)

Enclose quotations within a short quotation not set off from the text in single quotation marks. If the quotation ends the sentence omit the period in the sentence and place the period after the reference citation.

Isaacson relates that "Einstein was so exhausted when he finished a draft in June that his 'body buckled and he went to bed for two weeks'" (135).

Punctuation depends on the position of the quotation in the sentence.

Comma:

"My papers are much appreciated," Einstein exulted to Solovine.

Question mark:

"Would there be any point in my stressing my scientific papers on that occasion?" asked Einstein when he applied for a professorship.

Exclamation point:

"If only I could have looked on!" Einstein exclaimed when he heard of Elsa's intervention.

Punctuation of original quotations are placed inside quotation marks.

"Give me liberty or give me death!"

"Some men see things as they are and say, "Why?" I dream of things that never were and say, "Why not?"

ELLIPSIS

When omitting words, phrases or sentences from quoted material, insert three periods. Leave a space before the first, between each, and after the last.

ELLIPSIS IN THE MIDDLE OF A QUOTED SENTENCE

Describing the the views of Western and non-Western nations about ethnic cleansing, Michael Wines states, "But to many other nations, the Kosovo atrocities . . . were just the broken eggs of yet another national omelet, and the West was a self-righteous, ever-more meddlesome cook."

ELLIPSIS AT THE END OF A QUOTED SENTENCE

End the sentence with a period. Add three periods with a space between each. Leave no space before the final quotation mark.

Describing the views of Western and non-Western nations of ethnic cleansing, Michael Wines writes, "But to many other nations, the Kosovo atrocities that Germany equated with its own past and President Clinton labeled 'vicious' and "terrifying' were just the broken eggs of yet another national omelet. . . ."

ELLIPSIS AT THE END OF A QUOTED SENTENCE FOLLOWED BY A PARENTHETICAL REFERENCE

Leave a space after the last word. Insert three spaced periods followed by the closing quotation marks. Place the reference in parentheses and end with a period.

Describing the views of Western and non-Western nations of ethnic cleansing, Michael Wines writes, "But to many other nations, the Kosovo atrocities that Germany equated with its own past and President Clinton labeled 'vicious' and "terrifying' were just the broken eggs of yet another national omelet . . ." (91-92).

NUMBERS

In general use arabic numerals for all numbers not spelled out, except for the occasional use of roman numerals.

- Spell numbers of one or two words.
  three one thousand five million

- Use numerals for numbers of more than two words.
  3.56 2,456 1,489, 602

- Use numerals for numbers which precede units of measurement.
  24 volts 121.5 megahertz, 6 centimeters

- Use numerals for numbers in comparisons of data.
  The July temperature ranged from 67 to 90.

- Use numerals with abbreviations, addresses, dates, page numbers, and decimal fractions.
  12 lbs. $10.00 316 5th Avenue page 3
  April 21, 1929 9.5

- Use a combination of numerals and words for large numbers.
  4.7 billion dollars

- Use capital roman numerals in outlines and after names of individuals
  Henry VIII Richard III Topic III

- Use lowercase roman numerals for pages of a book which are numbered in roman numerals.
  page iv.. .page iii

- ..In divisions
  page 19 section 8 of the report

Use roman numerals in outlines and after person's names.

King Carlos II Richard Robbins III

MLA FORMATTING

PAPER

Use only high quality white paper 81/2 x 11 inches

MARGINS

In Word 2007 click on the Page Layout Tab. Click on the Margin icon. Select Normal with 1 inch margins all around.

PAGE NUMBERS WITH YOUR NAME FLUSH RIGHT

Click on the Insert Tab. Click on Page Number, Top of Page, and Plain Number 3. The number 1 will appear flush right 1/2 inch from the top of the page. Type your last name. Highlight your name and the page number and change the font to the one you select. Change the size to 12 point.

TYPE FONT AND SIZE

Select an appropriate type face such as Times New Roman, Arial, or similar easily read type in 12 point size.

HEADING

The MLA requires a simple heading instead of a title page. Beginning at the top margin, one inch down from the top of the paper, type your name, teacher's name, course name and number, and date double spaced flush left

TITLE

Center the title double spaced after the heading in the same font and size as all text. Capitalize only major words but not conjunctions and prepositions

FIRST LINE INDENT

Click on View and Ruler. The ruler will appear at the top of the page. Move the top inverted triangle to the 1/2 inch mark on the ruler to indent the first line of each paragraph.

LINE SPACING

Place the cursor in a paragraph. To double space press Ctrl+2 or click on the Home Tab and Paragraph button. Select double space in the dialog box.

See the sample first page on the next page.

SAMPLE MLA FIRST PAGE

1/2"

O'Brian 12

1"

Mary K. O'Brian

All text is double spaced

Mr. J. Smith, Instructor

Social Studies 12-10

8 May 2009

Health Care Reform – A Universal Health Care System

Many people believe that health care is a basic human right. Virtually everyone on the planet will contract illnesses, minor to life threatening, throughout their lives.

1" Therefore, plans should be made for the prevention of disease to keep people healthy and for an economically sustainable program to provide care for all regardless of ability to pay. A civilized society does not allow indigents to suffer and die. Although most 1" citizens would subscribe to these beliefs, the question before America is how to design such a health care system in a capitalist economic system.

1/2 " indent

The United States spends more on health care than anyone "but unfortunately the quality of care is going down," according to Health and Human Services Secretary Kathleen Sebelius in a conference call to reporters. Many Americans who do not have private physicians use the hospital emergency rooms for even minor illnesses creating crowded conditions at great cost. Even those who have insurance frequently find that it is insufficient to cover treatments. An article in the NY Times (Abelson, A12) stated that three quarters of those bankrupted by medical problems had insurance when they became ill.

Unfortunately, there are competing forces in Congress. Many oppose a single payer, government financed program that would compete with private insurers. Others are concerned about the tremendous costs of a universal system. However, at least one country, Israel, has health care that combines public and private sponsorship.

FIRST PAGE

Note the simple heading instead of a title page. Every page must have a header combining your name and the page number flush right one half inch from the top. Margins are one inch on all sides.

SAMPLE MLA TABLE

O'Brian 6.

Employer-sponsored health insurance premiums have nearly doubled since 2000, a rate three times faster than wages. In 2008, the average premium for a family plan purchased through an employer was $12,680, nearly the annual earnings of a full-time minimum wage job. Americans pay more than ever for health insurance, but get less coverage. Table1. shows the problems facing families in five selected states.

Table 1

Health Insurance Coverage in Five Selected States

States	Uninsured	Insured by Employee	Premium Cost	Increase Since 2000
NY	14%	21 million	$14,000	97%
FL	21%	9.8 million	$12,780	88%
CA	19%	19 million	$13, 297	114%
IL	14%	8.1 million	$13,631	89%

Source: United States, Dept. of Health and Human Services; *Hidden Costs of Health Care*, July 2009; Web; 11 Aug. 2009.

TABLES

Insert tables close to the text about the table. Type the word, Table, with an arabic numeral flush left. Double space and type the title of the table. Capitalize the title like a book title leaving prepositions and conjunctions in lower case. Double space the entire table. Use horizontal lines to separate parts, but avoid vertical lines. Type the source immediately below the table.

MLA WORKS CITED PAGE

O'Brian 9

Works Cited

Albelson, Reed. "Insure, but Bankrupted by Health Crises." *New York Times* 30 June 2009, late ed.: A1+. Print.

Dranove, David. *Code Red: An Economist Explains How to Revive the Healthcare System Without Destroying It.* Princeton: Princeton U P, 2008. Print.

Halvorsen, George C. *Epidemic of Care: A Call for Safer, Better, and More Accountable Health Care.* San Francisco, CA: Jossey-Bass, 2003. Print.

Kronke, Charles, and Ronald White. "The Modern Health Care Maze." *Independent Review* 14.1 (2009): 45-47. Print.

Pressman, Aaron. "How to Play It: Health-Care Reform." *BusinessWeek* 6 July 2009: 56. Print.

Reid, T. R. *The Healing of America.* New York: Penguin Press, 2009. Print.

Sessions, Samuel Y. and Allan S. Detsky. "Employment and US Health Care Reform. Saving Jobs While Cutting Costs." *Journal of the American Medical Association* 301.17 (2009: 1811. Print.

Twedt, Steve. "Official: U.S. Health Costs Up, Quality Down." *Pittsburgh Post-Gazette,* 27 June 2009. Web. 15 July 2009.

Whitesides, John. "Congress Back To Wrestle With Healthcare Reform." *Reuters,*. 6 July 2009. Web. 12 Aug. 2009.

WORKS CITED PAGE

This is the last page of the paper. Begin on a new page and continue the pagination. Center the title, Works Cited, one inch from the top. Double space and begin entries. Second and additional lines are indented five spaces or one inch.

APA

APA Manual 6th Edition 2009

PARENTHETICAL AUTHOR-DATE CITATION

The author's name and the date of the work are placed in parenthesis in the text. When the author's name appears in the text only the date needs to be placed in the parenthesis. A little practice may be necessary to insert the citation and keep the writing fluent.

PUNCTUATION OF AUTHOR-DATE CITATIONS

Parenthetical citations may be placed anywhere in the sentence, but be sure to maintain a smooth writing style, inserting the citation at a natural pause in thought. When both the author's name and date appear in the parenthesis, separate them with a comma.

REFERENCE LIST

Every source cited in the text must be documented in a Reference List at the end of the paper. It is important that references be cited accurately to permit readers to find and use the sources.

APA PARENTHETICAL AUTHOR-DATE CITATION

ONE WORK - SINGLE AUTHOR

Insert last name of author and year of publication in parentheses in the text.

A study of reactive inhibition (Smith, 2009) indicated

or

If author's name appears in text, insert only the year of the work in parentheses.

Smith's (2009) study of reactive inhibition indicated

In a second or later mention of same work within a paragraph, the year may be omitted if there will be no confusion.

In his study of reactive inhibition, Smith also found

If the parenthetical citation occurs at the end of a sentence, do not punctuate the sentence. Leave a space, add the citation and the end punctuation. Separate author and date within the parenthesis with a comma.

The results of the study of reactive inhibition were surprising (Smith, 2009).

ONE WORK - TWO AUTHORS

Mention of a work by two authors should always include both names separated by an ampersand *(&)* in the parentheses and the word, *and,* in the text.

Describing the many manifestations of mental disorder, (Rogers & Phillips, 2008) stated

Rogers and Phillips (2000) studied mental disorder

ONE WORK - THREE TO FIVE AUTHORS- FIRST CITATION

First mention of a work by three to five authors should include all the authors separated by an ampersand (&*)* in the parenthesis and the word, *and,* in the text.

Published studies that illustrate the P technique (Cattel, Cattel & Rhymer, 2009) stress the relationship

Published studies by Cattel, Cattel and Rhymer (2009) that illustrate the P technique

APA PARENTHETICAL AUTHOR-DATE CITATION

ONE WORK - THREE TO FIVE AUTHORS- LATER CITATION

In a later mention of a work by three to five authors cite only the last name of first author and the Latin abbreviation, et al. (not italicized and with a period after al) and the year only if it is the first citation of the reference within a paragraph.

In a study of P technique, Cattel et al. (2000) discovered

In a second or later mention of same work within a paragraph, the year may be omitted if there will be no confusion.

Cattel et al. discovered

If two different references of more than three authors shorten to the same citation; e.g.,

Richards, Bray, Hoe, Key, & Rogers, 2009
Richards, Bray, Smith, & Powers, 2009

Cite the last names of as many authors necessary to clarify.

Richards, Bray, Hoe, et al. (2009)
Richards, Bray, Smith, et al. (2009)

ONE WORK - SIX OR MORE AUTHORS

For a work with six or more authors, cite only the last name of the first author followed by et al. and the year for the first and subsequent citations.

Smith, et al. (1999) investigated

WHEN REFERENCES WITH MULTIPLE AUTHORS SHORTEN TO THE SAME FORM

Cattel, Cattel, and Rhymer (2000)
Cattel, Smith, and Cohen (2000)

Both citations above would both shorten to:

Cattel et al.(2000)

To avoid confusion, cite the last name of the first author and as many authors following as required to differentiate the two references.

Cattel, Cattel, et al. (2000)
Cattel, Smith, et al. (2000)

APA PARENTHETICAL AUTHOR-DATE CITATION

CORPORATE, GOVERNMENT AGENCY, ASSOCIATION AUTHORS

The names of associations, government agencies, and organizations, should usually be spelled out in a text citation each time they appear. If the abbreviation for the name of the association or agency is well-known, you can abbreviate it in later citations, but show the abbreviation in the first citation.

Statistical reports on mental illness in the armed forces (National Institute of Mental Health [NIMH], 2008) indicated

WORK - NO NAMED AUTHOR

In the text use the first few words of the reference list entry which will probably be the title and date for the citation. Use double quotation marks around titles of chapters, articles, or Web pages. Italicize the titles of books or periodicals.

Latest study of the brain reveals new understandings of brain waves ("New Brain Study," 2007).

in the book, Internet Research Projects (2009)

WORK - ANONYMOUS AUTHOR

Cite the work with the word Anonymous in the text and reference list.

(Anonymous, 2001)

AUTHORS WITH THE SAME LAST NAME

Include the initials of authors in the text citations.

The studies of J.A. Cohen (2006) and R. Cohen (2008) described

MULTIPLE WORKS - SAME AUTHOR(S) - SAME PARENTHESES

Arrange parenthetical citations in alphabetical order as they appear in the reference list. Include the dates in order of publication. List "in press" last. Do the same in reference list.

a few studies found (Branson, 1999, 2000, in press)

If author has two or more works published same year, add a lower case letter to the year.

The research revealed (Godlinson 2008a, 2008b)

APA PARENTHETICAL AUTHOR-DATE CITATION

MULTIPLE WORKS - SAME AUTHOR(S) - SAME DATES SAME PARENTHESES

With two or more works published same year, add a lower case letter to the year.

a few studies (Newman, 1999a, 1999b, 1999c)
a few studies (Jones & Crutch, 2000a, 2000b)

WORKS - MULTIPLE AUTHORS - SAME PARENTHESES

Cite the authors in alphabetical order. Separate names with semi-colons.

a few studies (Brown, 2000; Schwartz, 2001)

CLASSICAL WORK

For very old works, cite year of the version used followed by version.

Aristotle (1922 Version)

CLASSICAL WORK - TRANSLATED

Cite the name of the author followed by "trans." and the year of the translation.

(Plato, trans. 1967)

RELIGIOUS WORKS

Cite the version used.

1 Samuel 26 (King James Version)

CLASSICAL WORK - PLAYS, POEMS, BIBLE, ETC.

Cite the book, chapter, act, line, verse, canto, etc. of the work instead of page numbers because the numbering is the same regardless of edition.

As Shakespeare states (Hamlet, Act III, Scene i, lines 56-90)

PERSONAL COMMUNICATIONS

Cite e-mail, electronic discussion group or electronic bulletin board messages, phone conversations, personal interviews, etc. by stating the initials, last name of the source and date. Do not include in reference list.

R. Bronston (personal communication, January 21, 2009)
or (R. Bronston, personal communication, January 21, 2009)

APA PARENTHETICAL AUTHOR-DATE CITATION

CITING MULTIPLE ENTRIES BY SAME AUTHOR

List the earliest year of publication first

Johnson, P.R. (2005)
Johnson, P.R. (2006)

CITING MULTIPLE ENTRIES BY SAME AUTHOR AND OTHERS

List the individual author's work first.

Johnson, P.R. (2005)
Johnson, P.R., & Greenberg, S.R. (2005)

CITING MULTIPLE ENTRIES BY SAME AUTHOR AND DIFFERENT SECOND OR THIRD AUTHORS

Alphabetize by the last name of the second author. If the second author is the same, use the last name of the third author.

Johnson, P.R., & Greenberg, S.R. (2005)
Johnson, P.R., Tarshish, K.P., & Jones, G. (2004)
Johnson, P.R., Tarshish, K.P., & Zelon, B. (2006)

CITING WORKS PUBLISHED IN DIFFERENT YEARS BY SAME AUTHOR(S)

Insert lowercase letters a, b, c, etc after the year within parenthesis

Cornowon, B.K. (2002a)
Cornowan, B.K. (2002b)

THE REFERENCE LIST

A reference list called, References, is double spaced at the end of the paper. Sources that appear in the text must appear in the reference list. Accuracy is essential. Do not list personal communications such as e-mail, interviews, and letters.

Entries are alphabetized letter by letter by author's last names, an association name, or work title if the author is not known. Entries beginning with numerals are listed with the numerals spelled out. Always replace roman numerals with arabic numerals except when they are part of a title. Entries are double spaced with the first line at the margin and following lines indented one half inch.

PUBLISHER'S ADDRESSES IN THE REFERENCE LIST

Cite the city and state for U.S. publishers. Cite city, state, province or state, and country for non U.S. publishers. Do not repeat the state or province of university publishers if the state is included in the name. Names of cities that are major publishing centers may be cited without the state names. Use the U.S. Postal Service two letter abbreviations.

ELECTRONIC LOCATOR INFORMATION URL AND DOI

Today a great many sources are retrieved electronically. There are now two systems for retrieval: The Internet uses URLs to identify locations and a new system uses Digital Object Identifiers (DOIs).

The DOI system manages information on digital networks. The Digital Object Identifier (DOI) System provides current information, including where sources can be found on the Internet. Information about a digital object may change over time, including where to find it, but its DOI name will not change.

Each article is assigned an identifier and routing system. The DOI is like a URL. Each DOI begins with a 10 and contains a prefix of four or more digits assigned to organizations. The suffix is assigned by the publisher. The prefix and suffix are separated by a slash (/). The APA recommends that DOIs be included in references for print and electronic sources when available.

Cite the DOI if it has been assigned or the home page URL. Always copy-paste URLs and DOIs because they are usually long. Only divide URLs after slashes or other punctuation if necessary. Do not insert your own hyphens.

Do not include Retrieval dates unless the material may change.

SAMPLES ARE SINGLE SPACED TO SAVE SPACE.

PERIODICALS

JOURNAL ARTICLE WITHOUT DIGITAL OBJECT INDENTIFIER

Italicize the title of journals and the volume number. Capitalize only the first word of article titles and sub-titles. Italicize the volume number.

Linebarger, I. (2001). Learning to read from television: The effects of using captions and narration. *Journal of Educational Psychology, 93,* 288-298.

JOURNAL ARTICLE WITH DOI

Linebarger, I. (2001). Learning to read from television: The effects of using captions and narration. *Journal of Educational Psychology, 93,* 288-298. doi:10.1011/0356-4120.13.2.134

JOURNAL ARTICLE - TWO AUTHORS
JOURNAL PAGINATED BY ISSUE

Include the issue number in parentheses following the volume number only if each issue begins with page 1. Italicize the volume number but not the issue number.

Church, A., & Waclawski, J. (2001). A five-phase framework for designing a successful multisource feedback system. *Consulting Psychology Journal: Practice and Research, 53*(2), 82-85.

JOURNAL ARTICLE - UP TO SEVEN AUTHORS

Cite all authors' names with last name first followed by initials.

Jackson, K., Sher, J., Gotham, H., & Wood, P.K. Caruthers, P.K. (2001). Transitioning into and out of large-effect drinking in young adulthood. *Journal of Abnormal Psychology, 110,* 378-391.

JOURNAL ARTICLE - MORE THAN SEVEN AUTHORS WITH DOI

Cite all authors' last name first, initials. After next to last author insert three spaced periods and add the last author's name and the date of publication.

Eisenberg, N., Losoya, S., Fabes, R. A., Guthrie, I. K., Reiser, M., Murphy, B., Joshan, G. A., . . . Cohen, B. et al. (2001). Parental socialization of children's dysregulated expression of emotion and externalizing problems. *Journal of Family Psychology, 15,* 183-205. doi:10.1034/137980100067234

JOURNAL ARTICLE IN PRESS

Schwartzman, K., & Bennett, T. (in press). Leadership traits and team success. *Journal of Applied Psychology.*

SPECIAL ISSUE OR SPECIAL SECTION IN A JOURNAL

State the names of the editors and the title of the issue. Cite the page range for special sections.

Borowitz, C. & Zanit, R.P. (Eds.) (2008). Pandemics in third world countries [Special Issue]. *World Economic Trends, 51,* 21-26.

If no editors, cite the title first followed by a period before publication year. Alphabetize by first important word in title.

"Death Penalty - U. S." (2006). [Special Section] *Innocence Project Reports,* ***20,*** 211-12.

In text use a shortened title enclosed in quotation marks within the parenthesis.

("Death Penalty," 2006).

For articles in special issues, follow format for a journal article.

MAGAZINE ARTICLE

Insert volume number if one exists after the magazine name.

Bernstein, A. (2005, July 30). Racism in the workplace. Newsweek, 64-67.

ONLINE MAGAZINE ARTICLE WITH URL

Begley, S. (2009, July 1). What did Einstein know, and when did he know it? *Newsweek.* Retrieved from http://www.newsweek.com/id/204892

DAILY NEWSPAPER ARTICLE

Use p. for single pages and pp. for multiple pages.

Barron, J. (2008, August 1). Stem cells are used to produce insulin. *The New York Times*, p. A12.

DAILY NEWSPAPER ARTICLE - NO AUTHOR

Subway crash causes mental distress. (2001, August 1). *The New York Times,* p. A12.

Use shortened title for parenthetical citation in the text.

("Subway Crash," 2001).

NEWSLETTER ARTICLE - NO AUTHOR

Alphabetize by first important word in title.

School authorities may expel student. (2006, June). *Appellate Decisions Noted, 7*(8), 12-13.

In text use shortened title or full title if short enough in quotation marks within the parenthesis.

("School May Expel," 2006).

MONOGRAPH WITH ISSUE NUMBER AND SERIAL (OR WHOLE) NUMBER

For monographs with issue (or whole) number, insert the issue number in parenthesis followed by the serial number. *53*(2, Serial No. 201).

Coswell, R., & Klingenstein, P.R. (1965). A computer model of personality. Psychological Monographs, 79(1, Serial No. 540).

MONOGRAPH BOUND SEPARATELY AS JOURNAL SUPPLEMENT WITH DIGITAL OBJECT IDENTIFIER DOI

Cite the issue number and supplement or part number in parentheses after the volume number.

Johnson, P.Q., & Pritchard, K. (1969). Creativity. *Journal of Experimental Psychology Monographs, 80*(1, Pt. 2). doi:10.1027/0031-7920.35.1

EDITORIAL UNSIGNED

Editorial: Climate crisis. [Editorial]. (2009). *The New York Times,* p. A21.

ABSTRACT AS ORIGINAL SOURCE

Abstracts can be used in the reference list although it is preferable to use the full text of the article.

Petersen, S., Josephson, R. K., & Baronei, L. S. (2008). Issues in affirmative action. [Abstract]. *Research in Higher Education Abstracts. 21,* 112-114.

BOOKS - REFERENCE BOOKS BOOK CHAPTERS

BOOK - NO AUTHOR OR EDITOR

Alphabetize by first important word in title.

Psychology and you. (2005). New York: Macmillan.

BOOK

Insert editions, volume numbers, page numbers in parentheses following the title.

Helmstadter, G.C. (2004). *Research concepts in human behavior* (3rd ed.).San Francisco: Jossey-Bass.

ELECTRONIC VERSION OF PRINT BOOK WITH URL

Fitzgerald, F. S. (1925). *The great Gatsby* [eBooks@Adelaide version]. Retrieved from http://ebooks.adelaide.edu.au/f/fitzgerald/f_scott/gatsby/

BOOK - EDITED

Feigenbaum, E., & Feldman, J. (Eds.). (2003). *Computers and the new mind.* New York: McGraw-Hill.

BOOK - REVISED EDITION

Robertson, J. (2006). *Contemporary issues in psychology* (Rev. ed.). New York: Praeger.

APA REFERENCE LISTS

ARTICLE OR CHAPTER IN AN EDITED BOOK

Compton, J.P. (2008). Distance learning for teaching advanced placement courses in small high schools. In K.P. Slimes & R. Rogers (Eds.), *The Technological Explosion in Educational Practice* (pp. 207-208). New York: Knopf.

ARTICLE OR CHAPTER IN AN EDITED BOOK WITH DOI

Compton, J.P. (2008). Distance learning for teaching advanced placement courses in small high schools. In K.P. Slimes & R. Rogers (Eds.), *The Technological Explosion in Educational Practice* (pp. 207-208). New York: Knopf. doi:10.1037/10893-012

VOLUMES IN MULTIVOLUME EDITED WORK

Campanella, B. (Ed.). (1991-1999). *Schizophrenia: A history* (Vols. 1-9). New York: Knopf.

In text cite only the author(s) and dates in parentheses.
(Campanella, 1991-1999).

BOOK - GROUP AUTHOR OR GOVERNMENT AGENCY

When publisher and author are the same, use the the word, Author, as the name of the publisher.

American Psychological Association. (2009). *Publication Manual of the American Psychological Association* (6th ed.). Washington, DC: Author.

REFERENCE WORK

Johnson, R.S. (2002). Radioactivity. In *The new encyclopedia britannica* (Vol. 26). Chicago: Encyclopedia Britannica.

ONLINE REFERENCE WORK

solecism. (2009). In *Merriam-Webster Online Dictionary.* Retrieved from http://www.merriam-webster.com/dictionary/solecism

ONLINE REFERENCE WORK - NO AUTHOR

Fugitive Slave Act 1850. (n.d.). In *The Avalon project of Yale Law School.* Retrieved from http://avalon.law.yale.edu/19th_century/fugitive.asp

TECHNICAL AND RESEARCH REPORTS PRINT AND ONLINE

ONLINE GOVERNMENT REPORT WITH GOVERNMENT AGENCY AS AUTHOR

United States Department of Health and Human Services, National Institutes of Health, National Cancer Institute. (n.d.). *Cancer advances in focus: Breast cancer.* Retrieved from http://www.cancer.gov/cancertopics/cancer-advances-in-focus/breast

GOVERNMENT REPORT WITH U. S. GOVERNMENT PRINTING OFFICE AS PUBLISHER

United States Public Health Service. (2005). *Statistical tables for medical research* (USPHS Publication No. 37). Washington, DC: U.S. Government Printing Office.

CORPORATE AUTHOR - TASK FORCE REPORT ONLINE

Massachusetts Bar Association, Drug Policy Task Force Report. (2009). *The Failure of the War on Drugs: Charting a New Course for the Commonwealth.* Retrieved from http://www.massbar.org/for-attorneys/publications/e-journal/2009/june/06-18/drug-policy-task-force-report

AUTHORED REPORT - NONGOVERNMENTAL ORGANIZATION

McWilliams, A. (2009). *The U.S. Market for Clean Technologies (Report Code: ENV011A). Retrieved from BCC Research website: http://www.bccresearch.com/report/ENV011A.html*

REPORT FROM INSTITUTIONAL ARCHIVE

Kaplan, G. (1999). *Alameda County [California] Health and Ways of Living Study, (Report 4432). Retrieved from National Archive of Computerized Data on Aging website: http://search.icpsr.umich.edu/NACDA/query.html?col=abstract&rq=0&nh=500&qt=nacda&op0=&rf=3&fl0=subject%3A&ty0=p&tx0=NACDA+II.&fl1=availability%3A&ty1=w&op1=-&tx1=restricted*

ISSUE BRIEF

Center for Studying Health System Change. (2008, November). *Rising rates of chronic health conditions* (Issue Brief No. 125). Washington, DC: Author.

MEETINGS AND SYMPOSIA

SYMPOSIUM NOT FORMALLY PUBLISHED

Schreiber, R. (2009, February). Co-evolution of immunoediting on oncogenesis during tumor formation. In *Role of Inflammation in Oncogenesis.* Symposium conducted at the Keystone Symposia on Molecular and Cellular Biology, Keystone, CO.

CONFERENCE PAPER ABSTRACT RETRIEVED ONLINE

Afonso, O. (2008). *Public Deficits and Economic Growth.* Paper presented at the UACES Conference on Exchanging Ideas on Europe, Edinburgh, UK. Abstract retrieved from http://www.uaces.org/events/conferences/papers/abstract.php?recordID=2

PROCEEDINGS PUBLISHED REGULARLY ONLINE

Use same format as for a periodical.

Brecht, M., Radics, V., Nieder, J. B., and Bittl R. (2009). Protein dynamics-induced variation of excitation energy transfer pathways. *Proceedings of the National Academy of Sciences 106.* doi:10.1073/pnas.0903586106

PROCEEDINGS PUBLISHED IN BOOK FORM

Use same format as for a book.

Cser, A. (2009). English purist tendencies in a comparative perspective. In R. W. McConchie, A. Honkapohja, & R. Tyrkkö (Eds.), *Selected Proceedings of the 2008 Symposium on New Approaches in English Historical Lexis* (pp. 36-40). Somerville: MA.

DOCTORAL DISSERTATIONS MASTER'S THESES

Most dissertations and master's theses are retrieved from commercial databases. ProQuest Dissertations and Theses database houses Dissertation Abstracts International (DAI), Master's Theses International, and American Doctoral Dissertations. Always cite the database from which you retrieve a dissertation or thesis. Cite the accession or order number in parentheses at end of reference. Some dissertations are retrieved from university archives via the Internet.

MASTER'S THESIS FROM COMMERCIAL DATABASE

Johnson, R. K. (2008). *Use of computer based instruction with economically deprived students* (Master's thesis). Available from ProQuest Dissertations and Theses database. (UMI No. 1546719)

DOCTORAL DISSERTATION FROM INSTITUTIONAL DATABASE

Zampposoni, A. J. (2006). *Three studies of charter schools in New York City* (Doctoral dissertation). Retrieved from http://www.bobcat.nyu.edu/primo_library/

DOCTORAL DISSERTATION FROM THE WEB

Herman, E. (1993). *Psychology as Politics: How Psychological Experts Transformed Public Life in the United States 1940-1970* (Doctoral dissertation, Brandeis University). Retrieved from http://www.theasa.net/dissertations/ university/brandeis_university/

DOCTORAL DISSERTATION ABSTRACTED IN *DAI*

Note change in italicizing.

Jepsonar, L. M. (2006). Crash injury studies in three scheduled airline crashes. *Dissertation Abstracts International: Section B. Sciences and Engineering, 66*(11), 3729.

REVIEWS AND PEER COMMENTARY

Last name, Initial of reviewer. (Date). Review Title [Review of *Title of Medium,* by First initial. Last Name of author, producer, etc.]. *Title of work in which review appears, vol. no.* URL OR DOI

BOOK REVIEW

Gibson, E. (2009, June 4). [Review of the book *Management Rewired: Your Best Bet?* by C. S. Gibson] BusinessWeek. http://www.businessweek.com/magazine/content/09_24/b4135073010157.htm

MOVIE REVIEW

Turan, K. (2009, July 2). [Review of *Public Enemies,* directed by Michael Mann]. National Public Radio. Retrieved from http://www.npr.org/templates/story/story.php?storyId=105899079

VIDEO GAME REVIEW NO AUTHOR

[Review of the video game *Fallout 3* produced by Vault-Tec, 2009]. (n.d.). Retrieved from http://www.gamefaqs.com/console/xbox360/home/939933.html

PEER COMMENTARY ON AN ARTICLE

Sebba, M. (1999). *Social factors do matter!* [Peer commentary on keynote article "Borrowing and shift-induced interference: contrasting patterns in French-Germanic contact in Brussels and Strasbourg"' by J. Treffers-Daller]. Retrieved from http://eprints.lancs.ac.uk/1244/

AUDIOVISUAL MEDIA

MOTION PICTURE

Place the name of major contributors first followed by their function in parentheses. Place the words, Motion picture, in brackets after the title. State the country where the picture was made and released and the name of the studio.

Markson, J. (Producer), & Cohen, K. (Director). (1995). *The golden touch* [Motion picture]. United States: MCA.

TELEVISION EPISODE FROM A SERIES

Use same format as for a chapter in a book. Cite writers and directors in author position and the producer in the editor position.

Carson, B. (Writer), & Benson, R. (Director). (2001). The story of myth [Television series episode]. In R. Rogers (Producer), *The language of life.* New York: WNET.

MUSIC RECORDING

In text cite side and band or track numbers after date.

Weill, K. (1936). Johnny Johnson. On [CD]. Chestnut Hill, MA: Erato.

VIDEO

Library of Congress. Producer. (2003). *The Chinese in California 1850-1925* [DVD]. Available from http://memory.loc.gov/ammem/award99/cubhtml/cichome.tml

PODCAST

Cooper, A. (Reporter). (2009, July 3). *AC360 Daily podscast* [Video podcast]. Retrieved from http://cnn.podcast.com/episode/40710197/15818/

INTERNET MESSAGE BOARDS ELECTRONIC MAILING LISTS ONLINE COMMUNITIES

Many people communicate through online groups such as blogs, newsgroups, discussion groups, and electronic mailing lists. Use extreme caution citing these sources. Information may not be of scholarly value and may not be available for retrieval. Avoid using sources that are not archived. Cite the "screen name" of author if real name is not available. Enclose the description of the form in brackets. Do not italicize the "thread" which is the subject line of the message.

MESSAGE POSTED TO NEWSGROUP ONLINE FORUM OR DISCUSSION GROUP

jencor...@gmail.com. (2009, June 4). Re: The Ovarian Cancer National Alliance expressed concern today that a study, released last week at the annual meeting of the American Society of Clinical Oncology in Orlando, Florida, asserts that early detection of recurrent disease using the CA125 test five months earlier does not make any difference in survival [Online forum comment]. Retrieved from http://groups.google.com/group/primary-peritoneal-cancer/browse_thread/thread/998810052dd91cbd#

MESSAGE POSTED TO AN ELECTRONIC MAILING LIST

Seldon, S. (2009, June 26). Re: The wind energy industry congratulates House Speaker Nancy Pelosi, Chairmen Waxman and Markey, and the entire House leadership for successfully adopting energy and climate legislation that includes a Renewable Electricity Standard [Electronic mailing list message]. Retrieved from http://www.awea.org/newsroom/releases/AWEA_Statement_on_Climate_Legislation_062609.html

BLOG POST

KevinMD. (2009, July 4). Re: How did Michael Jackson die and the medicine behind sudden cardiac death [Web log message].Retrieved from http://www.kevinmd.com/blog/

VIDEO BLOG POST

Saeidkermanshah. (2009, June 13). Re: Protest against fake elections, Tehran, Iran [Video file]. Retrieved from http://www.youtube.com/watch?v=nifgnonH-BU

ARCHIVAL DOCUMENTS AND COLLECTIONS

Archival material includes letters, manuscripts, documents of institutions and corporations, photographs, and personal possessions. They may be owned by an individual or housed in a university, library, or institution. The citation should enable the reader to locate the source. Include as much information as possible including file numbers or call numbers if available. Include square brackets to enclose information that does not appear on the documents.

COLLECTION OF LETTERS FROM AN ARCHIVE

Churchill, W. (1874-1965). Correspondence. Sir Winston Churchill Documents. Churchill College Archives Centre, Cambridge: UK.

LETTER FROM PRIVATE COLLECTION

Whitehead, K. (1901, July 7). [Letter to Richard Sloane]. Copy in possession of Roger Billings.

APA QUOTATIONS

QUOTATIONS OF FORTY WORDS OR FEWER

Run into text and set off with double quotation marks. If the quotation ends the sentence, place the punctuation mark after the parenthetical citation.

Richardson (1996) found "younger subjects learned three of the skills more rapidly than older subjects" (p. 29).

QUOTATIONS OF MORE THAN FORTY WORDS

Omit quotation marks. Begin the quotation on a new line indented one half inch or five spaces from the left margin. Type the quotation double spaced in a block. If more than one paragraph is quoted, indent the first line of each an additional half inch or five more spaces. Double space the entire quotation. Use double quotation marks to enclose any quotations within the block quotation. In block quotations insert final punctuation at the end of the sentence and before the parenthesis.

Richardson (1996) found the following:

> The younger subjects learned color selection, timing, and manipulation at a much faster rate than the older subjects. The largest difference in learning rate occurred in the timing skill. However, the older subjects performed better on tasks involving judgement.
>
> On the other hand, three of the older subjects subjects did not improve. (p.29)

QUOTATIONS WITHIN A QUOTATION

Use single quotation marks to set off a quotation within a short quotation. Use double quotation marks to set off a quotation in a block quotation of forty words or more.

Johnson stated, "The 'rate of change' was not affected by the temperature" (p.371).

If the quotation is in mid-sentence, cite the source in parentheses immediately after the quotation marks and finish the sentence.

After reviewing the study, Chancer (2008) found that "more subjects who exhibited the behaviors responded positively to prescription intervention" (p.39), than those who did not.

If the quotation ends the sentence, cite the source after the quotation marks and end with the proper punctuation after the parenthesis.

The study revealed that "more subjects responded to prescription intervention" (Chancer, 2008, p. 39).

APA QUOTATIONS

INSERTING MATERIAL IN A QUOTATION

Use brackets to enclose additions or explanations by someone other than the author.

Richardson (1996) found that ”younger subjects learned three of the skills [when body types were controlled] more rapidly than older subjects” (p. 29).

ELLIPSIS

When omitting words or phrases within a quoted sentence, use three periods with space before the first and a space after the last. Use four periods to indicate an ellipsis between two sentences. One period will end the sentence and be followed by three periods. Avoid ellipsis points before or after a quotation.

“Among soldiers, some . . . succeed in recording in prose or poetry the thrill and horror of their experience” (Schwartz, 1994, p. 318).

APA CAPITALIZATIONS

Capitalize the following:

First word in a complete sentence
The members of the family met.

Major words in headings and titles in body of text and tables.
The novel, Of Human Bondage

But capitalize only the first word of titles of works in reference lists, but capitalize the major words of publications.
Rogers, B. Q., (1995). Effects of aircraft noise on residents.

Journal of Noise Prevention, 5, 101-103.

Proper Nouns and Trade Names
African-American Microsoft

Nouns followed by numerals or letters that indicate a place in a numbered series
During Experiment 6

Refer to Table 4

The design of Experiment 7

But not common parts of books or tables
chapter 6 column 3

Test titles
Scholastic Aptitude Test
Minnesota Multiphasic Personality Inventory

Derived factors within a factor analysis followed by a number
Stress Factor 9 Situation 8

Variables and effects with multiplication signs
the Speed x Time equation

But

variables of speed and time

APA ABBREVIATIONS

Abbreviate the following:

Common terms not listed as abbreviations in Merriam-*Webster's Collegiate Dictionary*

HIV FBI NASA FDA IQ HIV

Terms frequently used in APA Journals

(MMPI) Minnesota Multiphasic Personality Inventory
(CR) conditioned response
(CS) conditioned stimulus

But do not abbreviate O, E, or S for observer, experimenter, or subject.

Measurement units with numeric values

44 cm 121 Hz 1300 ppm

Latin Abbreviations

Use Latin abbreviations in parenthetical copy and English translation in nonparenthetical copy.

e.g., for example i.e., that is
vs. versus cf. compare

Punctuation of Abbreviations

Use periods with initials of names, U. S. as an adjective, Latin abbreviations, and reference abbreviations.

A. J. Andrews U. S. Army i.e. Vol. 2

Do not use periods with state names, capital letter abbreviations and measurement abbreviations except for in. **for** inch **because of confusion with the word** in.

CA PA NIMH APA cm hr

Plurals of abbreviations

Add an *s* without an apostrophe.

IRAs Eds. vols.

But form plural of page by writing pp.

APA NUMBERS

NUMBERS EXPRESSED IN NUMERALS

For numbers 10 and above

15 years old   11th grade   12 columns

For numbers below 10 when comparing with numbers 10 and above

3 of 16 subjects failed
but
12 subjects in each of three groups
(Subjects and groups are not being compared.)

For numbers preceding measurement units

frequency 121.5 megahertz   6 cm

For numbers representing mathematical functions

the 3rd decile   3%   6 times as often

For numbers in dates, ages, sums of money, subjects in experiments, page numbers, and chapter numbers.

June 2, 2006   5 year olds $30.00   2hrs

For parts of books, tables and lists of four or more numbers

chapter 3   column 4   Table 7
3, 5, 7, and 9 trials   page 26

For all numbers in the abstract of an APA paper

NUMBERS EXPRESSED IN WORDS

For numbers below 10 that do not describe precise measurements or are grouped for comparison with numbers below 10

three columns   six words   two-dimensions
three subjects met with seven other subjects

For zero and one when words are more understandable and when not used with numbers 10 and above.

one time usage   zero sum game

For numbers that begin titles, headings, or sentences. Avoid beginning sentences with numerals

Three subjects responded   Fifty attempted

APA NUMBERS

NUMBERS EXPRESSED IN WORDS

For common fractions

one third of the group
three fourths of the subjects

For generally accepted usage of common terms

Seven Deadly Sins   Ten Commandments

NUMBERS EXPRESSED IN NUMERALS AND WORDS

For rounded large numbers and modifiers containing two numbers

4.7 million people	costs of 3.7 billion
sixty 12 year olds	first 11 parts

USE DECIMAL FRACTIONS

Use a zero before the decimal point with numbers less than 1

0.75 mm   0.37 cm

Except when then number cannot be greater than 1 as in levels of statistical significance

$p< .05$ $p< .01$

USE ORDINAL NUMBERS

Follow the rules above for cardinal numbers

USE COMMAS IN NUMBERS

Between groups of three digits in numbers above 1,000

3, 332   0002   499

and not after the following exceptions

page numbers	page 1211
temperatures	2000 degrees
binary digits	010011
frequencies	1950 hz
serial numbers	365890765

FORM PLURALS OF NUMBERS

Add s or es without an apostrophe

threes and fours	20s and 40s
sixes	1990s

APA FORMATTING

PAPER

Use only high quality white paper 81/2 x 11 inches

MARGINS

In Word click on the Page Layout Tab. Click on the Margin icon. Select Normal with 1 inch margins all around.

TYPE FONT AND SIZE

The APA prefers 12 point Times New Roman typeface.

FIRST LINE INDENT AND LINE LENGTH

Click on View and Ruler. The ruler will appear at the top of the page. Move the top inverted triangle to the 1/2 inch mark on the ruler to indent the first line of each paragraph. Do not justify any lines. Do not hyphenate at ends of lines.

LINE SPACING

Double space. In Word, place the cursor in a paragraph. Press Ctrl+2 or click on the Home Tab and Paragraph button. Select double space in the dialog box.

RUNNING HEAD AND PAGE NUMBER

The APA requires a "running head," which is a shortened title of the paper, flush left with the page number flush right on every page including the title page. Use Word's Create Running Heads function.

TITLE PAGE

Under the running head center the title about half way down the page. Double space and type your name. Double space and type your school, course name, and instructor's name.

ABSTRACT

Page 2 is an abstract. Type the word, Abstract, in upper and lower case centered at the top of the page under the running head. Summarize the paper. Abstracts vary from 150 to 250 words. Type the abstract as a single paragraph with no paragraph indentation.

APA TITLE PAGE

Running Head: HEALTHCARE REFORM 1

Health Care Reform – A Universal Health Care System

Mary K. O'Brian

Anderson College

May 2010

TITLE PAGE

The first page of text begins on page 3 under the running head. Double space under the running head and type the title in upper and lower case. Continue typing double spacing throughout the paper.

APA ABSTRACT PAGE

Running head: HEALTHCARE REFORM 2

Abstract

Many Americans are without adequate health care, yet we spend more than any other developed country. Even those who have health insurance frequently find they are not fully covered and many face bankruptcy as a result. Efforts to correct this situation through Congressional legislation have continued for decades, yet there has been no solution. A major political roadblock has been the conflict between those who favor a single payer, government funded insurance program and those who prefer a business centered approach. However, there are some countries in which a combination of business and government have been successful. This paper will explore how such consortiums work.

ABSTRACT PAGE

The APA requires an abstract page for articles submitted for publication. The abstract should be limited to 150 to 250 words that summarize your paper. If you plan to submit the paper for publication, consult with your instructor or advisor for detailed requirements.

APA FIRST PAGE

Running Head: HEALTHCARE REFORM 3

Health Care Reform – A Universal Health Care System

Many people believe that health care is a basic human right. Virtually everyone on the planet will contract illnesses, minor to life threatening, throughout their lives. Therefore, plans should be made for the prevention of disease to keep people healthy and for an economically sustainable program to provide care for all regardless of ability to pay. A civilized society does not allow indigents to suffer and die. Although most citizens would subscribe to these beliefs, the question before America is how to design such a health care system in a capitalist economic system.

The United States spends more on health care than anyone "but unfortunately the quality of care is going down," according to Health and Human Services Secretary Kathleen Sebelius in a conference call to reporters (Twedt, 2009). Many Americans who do not have private physicians use the hospital emergency rooms for even minor illnesses creating crowded conditions at great cost. Even those who have insurance frequently find that it is insufficient to cover treatments. An article in the NY Times (Abelson, 2009) stated that three quarters of those bankrupted by medical problems had insurance when they became ill.

Unfortunately, there are competing forces in Congress. Many oppose a single payer, government financed program that would compete with private insurers. Others are concerned about the tremendous costs of a universal system. However, at least one country, Israel, has health care that combines public and private sponsorship. The plan has been in existence for several years and appears to be working well with few of the conflicts now facing the United States.

APA FIRST PAGE

The first page of text is page 3 after the title and abstract. Margins are one inch on all sides. Author-date parenthetical citation is used throughout.

APA TABLE

Employer-sponsored health insurance premiums have nearly doubled since 2000, a rate three times faster than wages. In 2008, the average premium for a family plan purchased through an employer was $12,680, nearly the annual earnings of a full-time minimum wage job. Americans pay more than ever for health insurance, but get less coverage. Table1. shows the problems facing families in five selected states.

Table 1

Health Insurance Coverage in Five Selected States

States	Uninsured	Insured by Employee	Premium Cost	Increase Since 2000
NY	14%	21 million	$14,000	97%
FL	21%	9.8 million	$12,780	88%
CA	19%	19 million	$13, 297	114%
IL	14%	8.1 million	$13,631	89%

Source: United States, Dept. of Health and Human Services; *Hidden Costs of Health Care*, July 2009; Web; 11 Aug. 2009.

APA TABLE

Keep tables simple. Avoid vertical lines. Always keep the running head. Number the tables in arabic flush left. Double space and type the table title. Use horizontal lines to separate headings from the data in the table. Notes about the table are placed beneath.

Running head: HEALTHCARE REFORM 11

References

Albelson, R. (2009, June 30). Insure, but bankrupted by health crises. *New York Times*, pp. A1, A4.

Dranove, D. (2008). *Code red: An economist explains how to revive the healthcare system without destroying it.* Princeton: Princeton University Press.

Halvorsen, G. (2003). *Epidemic of care: A call for safer, better, and more accountable health care.* San Francisco: Jossey-Bass.

Kronke, C. & White, R. (2009). The modern health care maze. *Independent Review, 14*(1), 45-47.

Pressman, A. (2009, July 6). How to play it: Health-care reform. *BusinessWeek*, 56-57.

Reid, T. R. (2009). *The healing of America.* New York: Penguin Press.

Sessions, S. & Detsky, A.S. Employment and US health care reform: Saving jobs while cutting costs. *Journal of the American Medical Association, 301*(17), 1811.

Twedt, S. (2009, June 27). Official: U.S. health costs up, quality down. Retrieved from http://www.post-gazette.com/pg/09178/980176-28.stm#ixzz0JkSnEXQ2&D

Whitesides, J. (2009, July 6). Congress back to wrestle with healthcare reform. *Reuters*, Retrieved from http://news.yahoo.com/s/nm/20090706/ts_nm/us_usa_healthcare_congress

APA REFERENCES PAGE

Center the word, References, at the top of the page and type entries double spaced with a hanging indent of about five spaces. Continue regular pagination.

TURABIAN

A Manual For Writers 7th Edition 2007

FOOTNOTE OR ENDNOTE BIBLIOGRAPHY STYLE

Turabian, based on the *Chicago Manual of Style* offers either the footnote or endnote bibliography citation style as well as the parenthetical-reference list systems of citation. History, social science, and humanities departments favor the footnote or endnote style.

This book will illustrate only the footnote or endnote bibliography style. If you wish to use the parenthetical author-date style, you can turn to the APA section. Endnotes, while a bit easier to type, may not be acceptable in your department.

The first mention of a source in a footnote or endnote must contain the full bibliographic information including author's name, title, page numbers and complete publication information.

BIBLIOGRAPHY LIST

Every source cited in the text must be documented in a Bibliography at the end of the paper using the correct formats.

TURABIAN FOOTNOTES

Reference notes in the form of footnotes or endnotes are used to let the reader know the source of a statement you make in the text. For example, if you quote, summarize or paraphrase another writer's words you must cite the source. Footnotes and endnotes are indented about five spaces and are single spaced. Double space between footnotes and endnotes.

CONTENT NOTES

Content notes are used to amplify or comment on something you have written in the text, but feel that to include it in the text would disturb the line of thought. Content notes, when appropriately used, can enhance a paper, but they should be used sparingly.

NOTE NUMERALS

Note numerals are placed at the end of a sentence or if necessary at the end of a clause following the punctuation without a space. Number notes consecutively through out the text. The note numeral is raised a half space above the line and usually reduced in size in superscript format like this:

A weak economic environment is one of the factors that gives a despotic leader control.[2]

FOOTNOTES

Microsoft Word will automatically insert a superscript numeral for footnotes and simultaneously draw a separator rule about one third across the bottom of the page, and insert a superscript numeral under the separator rule where the footnote is to be typed. Type the correct bibliographic entry next to the numeral without a space as shown below.

A newer style is to type the note numeral in normal size on the line followed by a period and a space. Unfortunately, Microsoft Word can only insert superscript numbers. Examples of both styles are shown below.

---

1. Ricardo Jones, The Rise of Fascism (New York: Knopf, 2004), 19-20.

[1]Ricardo Jones, The Rise of Fascism (New York: Knopf, 2004), 19-20.

ENDNOTES

Microsoft Word will insert a superscript numeral after the last word and under the last line of your text. Type the correct bibliographic entry next to the numeral under the last line without a space. When the paper is finished, place the cursor at the first endnote entry, and space down to a new page. Type the heading, NOTES, centered at the top of the page. Leave two blank spaces. Continue the regular pagination of your text.

FIRST ENDNOTE OR FOOTNOTE FOR A SPECIFIC REFERENCE

The first mention of a source in a footnote or endnote must contain the full bibliographic information including author's name, title, page numbers and complete publication information to let the reader know where you found the information and to allow the reader find the source.

2. Richard Garibolo, The Definition of Research, (New York: Crestview Press, 2001), 27.

FOLLOWING ENDNOTE OR FOOTNOTE FOR THE SAME TITLE WITH NO REFERENCES BETWEEN

If a reference to the same title occurs with no other reference between the first citation and subsequent citations, use the Latin, Ibid. without underlining or italicizing.

First Citation

2. Richard Garibolo, The Definition of Research, (New York: Crestview Press, 2001), 27.

Citation of the Same Page with No References to Other Sources Preceding.

3. Ibid.

Citation of a Different Page With No References to Other Sources Preceding.

4. Ibid., 31.

FOLLOWING NOTE FOR THE SAME TITLE WITH DIFFERENT REFERENCES BETWEEN

Last name, *Shortened Title of Work,* Page Number(s).

7. Garibolo, Research,41.

ENDNOTE/FOOTNOTE - BIBLIOGRAPHY SAMPLES

BIBLIOGRAPHY

Type the word, Bibliography, centered at the top of the last page of your text or endnotes. Double space and begin to type your entries. Continue with regular pagination. Every source you consulted must have a full bibliographic entry. Bibliographies are alphabetized by last name(s) of authors, single spaced with a single blank space between each entry. First lines are flush left with following lines indented five spaces. When more than one author's name appears, only the first named author's name is inverted.

Page numbers should include the first and last pages of relevant material. When an article is continued at the back of a magazine only the first page should be stated.

BOOKS

BOOK - SINGLE AUTHOR

Note

1. First name Last name, *Title* (Publication City: Publisher, Date of publication), page number(s).

1. Arthur Cohenson, *Turmoil in Iraq* (New York: Longview Press, 2007), 19-21.

Bibliography

Last name, First name. *Title.* Publication City: Publisher, Publication Date.

Cohenson, Arthur. *Turmoil in Iraq.* New York: Longview Press, 1999.

PREFACE, FOREWORD, INTRODUCTION WRITTEN BY AN AUTHOR OTHER THAN THE AUTHOR OF THE WORK WHEN THE INTRODUCTORY PIECE IS MORE SIGNIFICANT THAN THE BOOK

Note

2. First name Last name, preface to *Title of Full Work,* by First name, Last name of author of full work (Publication City: Publisher, Date of publication), page number(s).

2. Robert Sanderson, foreword to *The American Story*, by Thomas Concerto (Chicago: Free Press Association, 2004), vi.

Bibliography

Last name, First name. Preface to *Title of Full Work,* by First name Last name of author of full work. Publication City: Publisher, Date of publication.

Sanderson, Robert. Foreword to *The American Story*, by Thomas Concerto. Chicago: Free Press Association, 2009.

BOOK WITH NAMED AUTHOR OF INTRODUCTION, PREFACE OR FOREWORD

Note

3. First name Last Name of author, *Title of Full Work,* with an introduction, preface, or foreword by First name Last name (Publication City: Publisher, Date of publication), page number(s).

3. Jane Austen, *Pride and Prejudice,* with an introduction by Anna Quindlen (New York: The Modern Library, 1995), vii.

Bibliography

Last name, First name of author. *Title of Full Work*. With an introduction, preface or foreword by First name Last name of foreword author. Publication city: Publisher, Date of publication.

Austen, Jane. *Pride and Prejudice.* With an introduction by Anna Quindlen. New York: The Modern Library, 1995.

BOOK - ANONYMOUS AUTHOR

Note

3. *Title* (Publication City: Publisher, Date of publication), page number(s).

3. *The Rage of War* (Portland, Oregon: Kronstad Press, 2002), 312-313.

Bibliography

Place in the alphabetical list by the first word excluding articles *The* and *A*. This entry would be in the alphabetical list under the letter R.

Rage of War. Portland, Oregon: Kronstad Press, 2002.

BOOK - TWO AUTHORS

Note

4. First name Last name and First name Last name, *Title* (Publication City: Publisher, Publication Date), page number(s).

4. Alvin Corrizoni and Carl Van De Griff, *Negative Effects of Radiation Therapy* (Chicago: University of Chicago, 2008), 291.

Bibliography

Last name, First name, and First name Last name. *Title.* Publication City: Publisher, Publication Date.

Corrizoni, Alvin, and Carl Van De Griff. *Negative Effects of Radiation Therapy.* Chicago: University of Chicago, 2001.

BOOK - THREE AUTHORS

Cite authors as listed on title page.

Note

3. First name Last name, First name Last name, and First name Last name, *Title* (Publication city: Publisher, Publication Date), page number(s).

3. John Johon, Richard Conte, and Elizabeth Nonear, *The Birth of a Democratic Nation* (New York: Little Brown, 1984), 75-76.

Bibliography

Last name, First name, First name Last name, and First name Last name. *Title*. Publication City: Publisher, Publication date.

Johon, John, Richard Conte, and Elizabeth Nonear. *The Birth of a Democratic Nation.* New York: Little Brown, 1994.

BOOK - FOUR OR MORE AUTHORS

Note

4. First name Last name of author listed first on title page of book et al., *Title* (Publication City: Publisher, Publication Date), page number(s) of citation.

4. Bernard C. Raffer et al., *New York in Financial Crisis* (New York: Harper, 2009), 312-313.

Bibliography

Do not use et al following the first name as in the footnote or endnote. Cite all the names in the order printed on the book's title page.

Raffer, Bernard C., Richard Friedman, Robert A. Baron, and Roger Collonis. *New York in Financial Crisis*. New York: Harper, 2009.

TWO OR MORE BOOKS - SAME AUTHOR(S) WITH NO INTERVENING CITATIONS

Bibliography

For the second and later entries, replace the name(s) with an eight space line by typing the underline key eight times followed by a period. Arrange later titles either chronologically or alphabetically by title.

Johnson, Richard. *Biological Roots*. New York: Norton, 2001.

________. *Study of Life.* New York: Norton, 2001.

ASSOCIATION - COMMISSION - INSTITUTION - OR SIMILAR ORGANIZATION AS AUTHOR

Note

3. Name of Association, *Title* (Publication City: Publisher, Publication Date), page number(s).

3. Aircraft Owners and Pilots Association, *Flight Safety Issues in 2009* (Washington, D.C.: Aircraft Owners and Pilots Association, 2009), 37.

Bibliography

Name of Association. *Title.* Publication City: Publisher, Publication Date.

Aircraft Owners and Pilots Association. *Flight Safety Issues in 2009.* Washington, D.C.: Aircraft Owners and Pilots Association, 2009.

BOOK - EDITOR OR TRANSLATOR IN PLACE OF AUTHOR

Note

5. First name Last name, ed. or trans., *Title* (Publication City: Publisher, Publication Date), page number(s).

5. Catherine P. Yok, ed., *Exercise Physiology for Disabled Adults* (Toronto: Lame Bird Press, 1999), 187-188.

Bibliography

Last name, First name, ed. or trans. *Title.* Publication City: Publisher, Publication Date.

Yok, Catherine P., ed. *Exercise Physiology for Disabled Adults*. Toronto: Lame Bird Press. 1999.

BOOK - WITH AUTHOR AND EDITOR OR TRANSLATOR

Note

3. First name Last name of author, *Title*, ed. or trans. First name Last name of editor or translator (Publication City: Publisher, Publication Date), page number(s). Do not use the plural eds. with more than one editor.

3. Joseph Banks, *Collected Works*, ed. Paul Tillitsen (New York: Knopf, 1993), 217.

Bibliography

Last Name, First Name. *Title.* Edited or Translated by First name Last name of editor, translator, or compiler. Publication City: Publisher, Date of publication.

Banks, Joseph. *Collected Works*. Edited by Paul Tillitsen. New York: Knopf, 1993.

BOOK - EDITOR AND TRANSLATOR PLUS AUTHOR

Note

6. First name Last name of author, *Title*, ed. First name Last name name of editor, trans. First name Last name of translator (Publication City: Publisher, Publication Date), page number(s).

Do not use plural eds. even if there are two editors.

6. Paul Szy, *Thoughts*, ed. Sam Smith, trans. May Clint (New York: Klaus, 2004), 31-34.

Bibliography

Last Name, First name of author. *Title.* Edited by First name Last name name of editor. Translated by First name Last name of translator. Publication City: Publisher, Publication Date.

Szy, Paul. *Thoughts.* Edited by Sam Smith. Translated by May Clint. New York: Klaus, 2004.

EDITIONS

Editions must be cited if the book is not a first edition. Follow exactly the designation the publisher has printed on the title page or copyright page but in abbreviated form. For example, if Third Edition, Revised is on the title page, the citation would be 3rd ed., rev.

Types of Editions and Citation Abbreviations

Second Edition-----------------------------------2nd ed.
Third Edition, Revised-------------------------3rd ed., rev.
Revised Edition-----------------------------------rev. ed.
New Revised Edition---------------------------new rev. ed.
Revised 3rd Edition----------------------------rev. 3rd ed.
Second Edition, Revised and Enlarged--2nd ed., rev. and enl.
Fourth Edition, Revised by Sam Sims--- 4th ed., rev. Sam Sims

BOOK IN AN EDITION

Note

2. First name Last name, *Title*, Xth ed. (Publication City: Publisher, Publication Date), page number(s).

2. Penelope Fink, *The Constitutional Convention,* 3rd ed. (Cleveland: Foxfire Press, 1984), 87-88.

Bibliography

Last name, First name. *Title*. Xth ed. Publication City: Publisher, Publication Date.

Fink, Penelope. *The Constitutional Convention*. 3rd ed. Cleveland: Foxfire Press, 1984.

REPRINT EDITIONS INCLUDING THOSE PUBLISHED AS PAPERBACKS OR IN ELECTRONIC FORM

Note

If reprinted by original publisher, (date of original publication; repr., Publication City: Publisher, reprint date), page number(s).

4. First name Last name, *Title* (Original Publication Date; repr., Publication City: Publisher, Publication Date) page number(s).

4. Nowland Van Powell, *The American Navies of the Revolutionary War* (1974: repr., New York: G.P. Putnam's Sons, 2005) 28.

Bibliography

Last name, First name. *Title.* Original Publication Date. Reprint, Publication City: Publisher, Publication Date.

Van Powell, Nowland. *The American Navies of the Revolutionary War.* 1974. Reprint, New York: G.P. Putnam's Sons, 2005.

ORIGINAL PAPERBACK EDITIONS

Note

Cite as any other book, but include the publisher's paperback designation if given.

2. First name Last name, *Title* (Publication City: Publisher, Publication Date, Paperback designation if any), page number(s).

2. Jay Toss, *Vengeance* (New York: Karman, 1999, Paperback Classics), 53.

ENDNOTE/FOOTNOTE - BIBLIOGRAPHY SAMPLES

BIBLIOGRAPHY

Last name, First name. *Title* (Publication City: Publisher, Publication Date, Paperback designation if any), page number(s).

Toss. Jay. *Vengeance* (New York: Karman, Paperback Classics, 1999).

BOOK IN A SERIES

Note

9. First name Last name, *Book Title*, Series Title (Publication City: Publisher, Publication Date), page number(s).

9. Rosetta Quinlin, *19th Century Drama,* American Theatre History (Chicago: Cornwall Press, 2008), 211-212.

Bibliography

Last Name, First name. *Book Title*. Series Title. Publication City: Publisher, Publication Date.

Quinlin, Rosetta. *19th Century Drama*. American Theatre History. Chicago: Cornwall Press, 2008.

PART OF A BOOK BY A SINGLE AUTHOR

Note

11. First name Last name, "Work Title," in *Title of book containing the work* (Publication City: Publisher, Publication date), page number(s).

11. Jocelyn Cruces, "Early Intervention," in *Psychiatric Care* (New York: Houghton Mifflin, 2009), 112.

Bibliography

Last name, First Name, "Work Title." In *Title of book containing the work* (Publication City: Publisher, Publication date.

Cruces, Jocelyn. "Early Intervention." In *Psychiatric Care*. New York: Houghton Mifflin, 2009.

MULTIVOLUME WORK - CITING ALL VOLUMES AS A WHOLE

Note

Include the total number of volumes in the citation and all publication dates if published over several years.

8. First name Last name, *Title*, X vols. (Publication City: Publisher, (Publication Date).

8. Richard Dennison, *Economic Trends,* 4 vols. (New York: Pace University Press, 1999-2003).

Bibliography

Last name, First name. *Title.* X vols. Publication City: Publisher, Publication Date.

Dennison, Richard. *Economic Trends.* 4 vols. New York: Pace University Press, 1998-2003.

WHOLE VOLUME OF A MULTIVOLUME WORK BY ONE AUTHOR WHEN EACH VOLUME HAS A DIFFERENT TITLE

Note

3. First name Last name, *Title of Multivolume Work*, vol. x *of Volume Title* (Publication City: Publisher, Publication Date), page number(s) of citation.

3. Richard Dennison, *Economic Trends,* vol. 2 of *Macroeconomics* (New York: Pace University Press, 1999), 125-126.

Bibliography

Last name, First name. *Title of Multivolume Work*. Vol. X, *Title of Volume X*. Publication City: Publisher, Publication Date.

Dennison, Richard. *Economic Trends*. Vol. 2 of *Macroeconomics.* New York: Pace University Press, 1999.

MULTIVOLUME WORK WITH A GENERAL EDITOR AND AN EDITOR FOR AN INDIVIDUAL VOLUME

Note

13. First name Last name of author, *Title of Individual Volume,* ed. First name Last name of editor, vol. x of *Title of Multivolume Work,* ed. First Name Last name of editor of multivolume work (Publication City, Publisher, Publication Date), page number(s).

13. Paul Larsen, *Economic Trends*, ed. Clark Kent, vol. 3 of *Inflation*, ed. Richard Dennison (New York: Pace University Press, 1999) 141-142.

Bibliography

Last name, First name of author, *Title of Individual Volume.* Edited by First Name Last Name of editor, Vol. X of *Title of Multivolume Work,* edited by First Name Last Name of editor. Publication City: Publisher, Publication Date.

Larsen, Paul, *Economic Trends*. Edited by Clark Kent, Vol. 3 of *Inflation*, edited by Richard Dennison. New York: Pace University Press, 1999.

WORKS IN ANTHOLOGIES

Note

9. First name Last name, "Poem Title," in *Anthology Title,* ed. First name Last name of editor (Publication City: Publisher, Publication Date) page number(s).

9. Nathalia Crane, "The Janitor's Boy," in *The New Modern American & British Poetry*, ed. Louis Untermeyer (New York: Harcourt, Brace, 1949), 260-61.

Bibliography

Last name, First name. "Poem Title." In *Anthology Title.* edited by First name Last name of editor. Publication City: Publisher, Publication Date.

Crane, Nathalia. "The Janitor's Boy." In *The New Modern American & British Poetry*, edited by Louis Untermeyer. New York: Harcourt, Brace, 1949.

WORKS IN EDITED COLLECTIONS

Note

11. First name Last name of author of work, "Title of Work," in *Title of Collection*, ed. First name Last name of editor (Publication City: Publisher, Publication Date), Page number(s).

11. Richard Schmidt and Carl Furgerson, "Totalitarianism in Modern China," in *Chinese History From 1900 to 2000,* ed. John Quarles (Chapel Hill: Carolina Press, 2005) 67-68.

BIBLIOGRAPHY

Last name, First name of author of work. "Title of Work." In *Title of Collection,* edited by First name Last name of editor, 12-14. Publication City: Publisher, Publication Date.

Schmidt, Richard and Carl Furgerson. "Totalitarianism in Modern China." In *Chinese History From 1900 to 2000*, edited by John Quarles, 12-14. Chapel Hill: Carolina Press, 2005.

JOURNALS - MAGAZINES - NEWSPAPERS

ARTICLE IN A SCHOLARLY JOURNAL WITH CONTINUOUS PAGINATION

Note

1. First name Last name, "Article Title," *Journal Title* Volume Number (Publication Date): page number(s).

1. Thomas R. Guskey, "What Makes Professional Development Effective?" *Phi Delta Kappan* 84 (2003): 748-750.

Bibliography

Last name, First name. "Article Title." *Journal Title* Volume Number (Publication Date): page number(s).

Guskey, Thomas R. "What Makes Professional Development Effective?" *Phi Delta Kappan* 84 (2003): 748-750.

ARTICLE IN A SCHOLARLY JOURNAL WITH EACH ISSUE NUMBERED AND PAGINATED SEPARATELY

Note

3. First name Last name, "Article Title," ***Journal Title*** **Volume Number, Issue Number (Publication Date): page number(s).**

3.James Moody, "Structural Cohesion and Embededness," *American Sociological Review* 68, no. 1 (2003): 103-107.

Bibliography

Last name, First name. "Article Title." ***Journal Title*** **Volume Number, Issue Number (Date): page number(s) of citation.**

Moody, James. "Structural Cohesion and Embededness." *American Sociological Review* 68, no. 1 (2003): 103-107.

GENERAL INTEREST MAGAZINES

Note

Identify by date alone. Do note use volume and issue numbers.

4. First name Last name, "Article Title," ***Magazine Name*****, Publication Date, page number(s).**

4. James C. Cooper, "The Skittish Bond Market," *Business Week,* July 14, 2003, 29-30.

Bibliography

Last name, First name. "Article Title." ***Magazine Name.*** **Publication Date, page number(s).**

Cooper, James C. "The Skittish Bond Market." *Business Week*, July 14, 2003.

REGULAR COLUMN OR DEPARTMENT IN A MAGAZINE

Note

12. First name Last name, Column or Department Title, ***Magazine Title,*** **Publication Date, page numbers(s).**

12. James Surowiecki, Financial Page, *New Yorker,* July 9, 2007, 40.

Bibliography

Last name, First name. Column or Department Title. *Magazine Title,* Publication Date.

Surowiecki, James. Financial Page. *New Yorker.* July 9, 2007.

NEWSPAPERS

Bibliography

References to newspapers are not usually included in bibliographies unless the article is needed to support an essential point in your paper.

EXTENSIVE REFERENCES TO NEWSPAPERS OR MAGAZINES

Bibliography

If many references to issues of the same periodical have been used in the paper, include the title and the dates of publication in a separate section of the bibliography.

***Periodical Title.* Dates of issues used in text.**

New Yorker. 7, 14, 28 June; 15, 22 July 2001.

NEWSPAPERS

Note

Page numbers are usually omitted from notes. Add edition if there is one after the publication date. Use either headline style or sentence style for article titles. This sample uses headline style with first letters capitalized.

6. First name Last name, "Title of Article," *Newspaper Name*, Month Day, Year, edition.

6. James Cronts, "Abbas in Clash Over His Stance in Peace Talks," *Nassau (NE) Times*, July 9, 2006, late edition.

NEWSPAPER NAMES

Do not use *The* in names of newspapers.

New York Times not *The New York Times.*

NEWSPAPER - U.S. - CITY OF PUBLICATION NOT IN NAME

Note

Add *city name* before newspaper name and add state in parenthesis if city is not easily identified

Binghamton Journal   *Clarkstown (IL) Bugle*

NEWSPAPER - FOREIGN - CITY OF PUBLICATION NOT IN NAME

Note and Bibliography

Add city name, not italicized, in parenthesis after the title.

Times (London)

NEWSPAPER - WELL KNOWN

Note

Omit publication city.

USA Today

Wall Street Journal

NEWSPAPER COLUMNS

When citing newspaper columns, use the column title, the column headline or both. Do not place the column title in quotation marks.

Note

5. First name Last name, "News story headline," Column Title, *Newspaper Name*, Publication Date.

5. N. Gregory Mankiw, "Fair Taxes? Depends on What You Mean by 'Fair,'" Economic View, *New York Times,* July 15, 2007.

LETTERS TO THE EDITOR

Do not use headlines when citing letters to the editor.

NOTE

3. First name Last name, letter to the editor, *Newspaper Name*, Publication Date.

3. Richard Hartwick, letter to the editor, *Wall Street Journal*, July 12, 2006.

NEWSPAPER SUNDAY MAGAZINE OR OTHER SUPPLEMENTS

Use the same bibliography and note entries as for magazine articles.

MEDIEVAL & EARLY ENGLISH WORKS

WORKS OF WELL-KNOWN AUTHORS

Note

Omit publication information. Cite only author, title, and appropriate divisions. Do not include in bibliography.

3. Author, *Title,* appropriate divisions.

3. Chaucer, *The Nun's Priest's Tale*, lines 70-75.

4. Spenser, *The Faerie Queen,* bk.1, canto 6, st.14.

WORKS OF WELL-KNOWN AUTHORS EDITED AND OR TRANSLATED

Note

For translations or edited editions or if your paper deals with literary criticism, add the source to your bibliography.

Treat as a translated or edited book.

5. Author, *Title*, ed. and trans. First name Last name of editor and or translator, (Publication City: Publisher, Publication Date), page number(s).

5. Chaucer, *Complete Works of Chaucer*, ed. and trans. Thomas Bennett (New York: Presidential Press, 1993), 61-62.

Bibliography

Author. *Title.* Edited and Translated by First Name Last Name. Publication City: Publisher, Publication Date.

Chaucer. Complete Works of Chaucer. Edited and Translated by Thomas Bennett. New York: Presidential Press, 1993.

CLASSICAL WORKS & SACRED TEXTS

CLASSSICAL WORKS

Use no punctuation between author, title, and section numbers.

7. Author Title Section numbers with no space between.

7. Aristotle *Antigone* 1.3

11. Plato *Apology* 212-213.

BIBLE

Note

Do not include in bibliography.

Abbreviated book name chapter number:verse (Version).

8. 2 Kings 8:5 (New Revised Standard Version).

3. Romans 9:13 (St. James Version)

OTHER SACRED WORKS

Note

Use punctuation similar to that for the Bible. Clarify with your instructor for specific works. Do not include in bibliography.

Work name Number:line number(s).

Qur'an 2:257.

PLAYS

WELL-KNOWN PLAYS

Well-known English language plays may be cited in notes only without bibliographic information. Cite only act and scene number

Note

4. First name Last name, *Play Title,* act x, scene y.

4. Tennessee Williams, The Glass Menagerie, act 2, scene 3.

PLAYS - OTHER

For translations, less well-known plays, or if your paper deals with literary criticism, use the same citations as for a book. Add the source to your bibliography as well. Cite either act and scene or page number.

Note

5. First name Last name, *Play Title*, (Publication City: Publisher, Publication Date), act x, scene y.

5. Tennessee Williams, *The Glass Menagerie*, (New York: French, 1944), act 2, scene 3.

Bibliography

Last name, First name. *Play Title*. Publication City: Publisher, Publication Date.

Williams, Tennessee. The Glass Menagerie. New York: French, 1944.

PERFORMANCES - LIVE

DANCE, THEATER, MUSIC WITH WORK TITLE PRIMARY

Note

Include work title, performers and significant others with roles, location and date of performance. Titles of short works are in roman type and set off in quotation marks. Do not include in bibliography unless the work is critical to your paper.

4. *Title of Play or Long Performance Title*, performer and role, Theater Name, Location, Performance Date.

4. *Travatore,* directed by Will Crutchfield, Caramoor, Katonah, New York, July 20, 2007.

7. *Gypsy,* directed by Arthur Laurents, vocal by Patti LuPone, New York City Center, New York, NY, July 15, 2007.

DANCE, THEATER, MUSIC WITH PERFORMER PRIMARY

Note

10. Stephanie Blythe, mezzo-soprano, *Third Symphony* by Gustav Mahler, Tanglewood, Lenox, MA, July 15, 2007.

PERFORMANCES - RECORDED

MOTION PICTURE

Note

It is best to cite a movie performance by including all the elements you need to mention in the text of your paper. If viewed in a theater cite it as a live performance of a play. Do not include in bibliography.

If the title of the movie is most important, cite it first. Otherwise, cite first whoever is deemed most important: producer, director, or other. If appropriate add any names or information relevant to the film. Include a scene description if necessary.

7. *Film Title,* producer, director, or other, Production Company, Year of Production.

7. *Capote*, produced by Caroline Baron, Sony Pictures Classics, 2005, execution scene.

SOUND RECORDING - MUSICAL

Note

Cite first the title or whoever is emphasized: composer, conductor, writer. If stated, the name of the performer follows the title. Include the name of the recording company and any identification numbers, the medium and copyright date or production date. Include in bibliography.

5. First name Last name, *Title of Recording*, performed by name(s) of artists, Recording company, Numbers if available, medium, copyright date if known.

5. Andrew LLoyd Webber, *Phantom of the Opera,* performed by Michael Crawford and Sarah Brightman, EMI, audiocassette, 1987.

Bibliography

Last name, First name. *Title of Recording.* Performed by First name Last name(s) of artist(s). Recording Company, Medium. Date. (if known).

Webber, Andrew Lloyd. *Phantom of the Opera*. Performed by Michael Crawford and Sarah Brightman. EMI. Audiocassette. 1987.

SOUND RECORDING - DRAMA, PROSE, OR POETRY, LECTURES

Note

3. First name Last name, *Title of Work*, performed by, Recording company, Medium, Date.

3. Sholem Aleichem, *Motl, the Cantor's Son*, read by Isaiah Sheffer, National Yiddish Book Center, CD, 2003.

Bibliography

Last name, First name. *Title of Work.* Performed by. Recording company. Type of recording. Date.

Aleichem, Sholem. *Motl, the Cantor's Son.* Read by Isaiah Sheffer. National Yiddish Book Center. CD. 2003.

VIDEO RECORDINGS

Note

Begin with First name Last name of writer or actor if appropriate.

7. *Title*, VHS or DVD,produced or conducted or directed by First name Last name (Production City, ST: Production Company, Production date).

7. *Monsoon Wedding,* VHS, produced by Mira Nair (Universal City, CA: Universal Studios, 2002).

Bibliography

***Title*. VHS or DVD. Produced or Conducted or Directed by First name Last name. Production City, ST: Production Company, Production date.**

Monsoon Wedding. VHS. Produced by Mira Nair Universal City, CA: Universal Studios, 2002.

TELEVISION AND RADIO PROGRAMS

Cite only in notes. Do not include in bibliography. Include as relevant: program title, date observed, episode title and number if obtainable, actors, television station or network, broadcast date.

Note

2. *Program Title*, "Episode Title," Episode number if known, Television Station
n or Network, Broadcast Date.

2. *Sopranos*, "Therapist," episode 41, HBO, October 26, 2006.

TELEVISION OR RADIO INTERVIEWS

Cite only in notes or incorporate the interview into your paper.

Note

10. First name Last name of Interviewee, interview by First name Last name of Interviewer, *Title of TV or Radio Program*, TV or Radio Station, Interview Date.

10. Laura Bush, interview by Larry King, *Larry King Live,* CNN, February 15, 2006.

TELEVISION OR RADIO ADVERTISEMENTS

Cite only in notes or incorporate the interview into your text.

Note

8. Franklin Templeton Investments, advertisement, aired during the British Open Golf Tournament, July 22, 2007.

REVIEWS

REVIEWS OF BOOKS AND PERFORMANCES IN A NEWSPAPER

Note

4. First name Last name of reviewer, review of *Work Title*, by First name Last name of work author, *Title of Publication in which review is published,* Publication Date.

4. Terrence Rafferty, review of *Specimen Days*, by Michael Cunningham, *New York Times*, June 26, 2006.

Bibliography

Do not include in bibliography unless the review is significant to your paper.

Last name, First name of reviewer. Review of *Book Title*, by First name Last name of book author, *Title of Publication*, Day Month Year of publication.

Rafferty, Terrence. Review of *Specimen Days*, by Michael Cunningham. *New York Times*, June 26, 2006.

REVIEW OF BOOKS AND PERFORMANCES IN A JOURNAL

Note

6. First name Last name of reviewer, review of *Book Title*, by First name Last name of book author, *Journal Title* Volume Number (Month Year of publication): page number(s).

6. Gerard Brossman, review of *Hebrides Rediscovered*, by Richard Roscommon, *Journal of Paleontology* 45 (November 1989): 212-213.

Bibliography

Do not include in bibliography unless the review is significant to your paper.

Last name, First name of reviewer. Review of *Book Title*, by First name Last name of book author. *Journal Title* Volume Number (Month Year of publication) page number(s).

Brossman, Gerard. Review of *Hebrides Rediscovered*, by Richard Roscommon, *Journal of Paleontology* 45 (November 1989).

UNSIGNED PLAY, FILM, OR PERFORMANCE REVIEW IN A NEWSPAPER

Note

1. Review of *Performance Title*, by First name Last name of performance author, (Name of Theater Company, City of Performance), *Name of Newspaper*, Month Day, Year of Publication.

1. Review of *Courage*, by Jason Krupps, The Aquila Theater Company, New York, *New York Times*, June 28, 2005.

ENDNOTE/FOOTNOTE - BIBLIOGRAPHY SAMPLES

Bibliography

Do not include in bibliography unless the review is significant to your paper.

Review of *Performance Title*, by First name Last name of author. Name of Theater Company. City of Performance. *Name of Newspaper*, Month Day, Year of Publication.

Review of *Courage*, by Jason Krupps. The Aquila Theater Company, New York. *New York Times*, June 28, 2005.

UNPUBLISHED SOURCES

INTERVIEW BY AUTHOR OF PAPER

Note

8. First name Last Name of Interviewee, interview by author, Day Month Year, Location, Type of recording if any.

8. Robert Lowelstein, interview by author, New York, NY, August 15, 2005.

Bibliography

Do not include in bibliography unless the interview is significant to your paper.

Last name, First name of Interviewee. Interview by author. Day Month Year, Location. Type of recording.

Lowelstein, Robert. Interview by author. New York, NY, August 15, 2005.

THESIS OR DISSERTATION

Note

22. First name Last name, "Thesis or Dissertation Title," (PhD diss., University, Date), Page number(s).

22. Roger Clementis, "The Computer Modeling of Aberrant Behaviors," (PhD diss., New York University, 1999), 44-45.

Bibliography

Last name, First name. "Thesis or Dissertation Title." Ph D diss., University, Date.

Clementis, Roger. "The Computer Modeling of Aberrant Behaviors." PhD diss., New York University, 1999.

SPEECHES, LECTURES, PAPERS AT MEETINGS

Notes

13. First name Last name, "Title of Speech or Paper" (lecture, speech, or paper, Meeting Location, City, ST, Month Day, Year).

13. Gregory Gross, "America's Green Power" (commencement address, Hamilton College, Clinton, NY, June 12, 2004.

Bibliography

Last name, First Name. "Title of Speech or Paper." Lecture, Speech, or Paper, Meeting Location, City, ST, Month Day, Year.

Gross, Gregory. "America's Green Power." Commencement address, Hamilton College, Clinton, NY, June 12, 2004.

ABSTRACTS - PAMPHLETS - REPORTS

ABSTRACTS

Notes

Do not include in bibliography unless significant for your paper.

3. First name Last name, "Article Title," abstract, *Journal Title* Volume Number, Issue Number (Publication Date): page number(s).

3. James Moody, "Structural Cohesion and Embededness," abstract, *American Sociological Review* 68, no. 1 (2003): 103-107.

PAMPHLETS AND REPORTS

Notes

Do not include in bibliography unless significant for your paper.

17. First name Last name or Organization, *Report Title* (Publication City, ST: Publisher, Publication date), page number(s).

17. Brooklyn College Alumni Association, *2006 Annual Report* (Brooklyn, NY: Brooklyn College Alumni Association, 2007), 27.

ART WORKS

SCULPTURE - PHOTOGRAPHS - PAINTINGS

Notes

Do not include in bibliography.

4. First name Last Name of Artist, *Title of Art Work*, Creation date include *ca.* if approximate, Institution housing artwork, Location.

4. El Greco, *Toledo*, ca. 1541-1614, Oppenheimer Collection, Metropolitan Museum of Art, New York, NY.

GOVERNMENT PUBLICATIONS

GOVERNMENT COMMISSIONS - REPORTS, BULLETINS, AND CIRCULARS

Use the abbreviation GPO for Government Printing Office

Note

1. Commission Name, *Title of Commission Report* (Washington, D. C. : GPO, Date), Page number(s).

1. U.S. Equal Employment Opportunity Commission, *Performance and Accountability Report FY 2004* (Washington, D.C.: GPO, 2004), 9.

Bibliography

U. S. Commission Name. Title of Commission Report. Washington, D. C. : GPO, Date.

U. S. Equal Employment Opportunity Commission. *Performance and Accountability Report FY 2004.* Washington, D. C.: GPO, 2004.

EXECUTIVE DEPARTMENT REPORTS, BULLETINS, AND CIRCULARS

Note

5. Department Name, Department Office, Bureau, or Agency, *Title of Report* (Washington, D. C., Date), Page number(s).

5. Department of Justice, Office of Justice Programs, *Mass Fatality Incidents: A Guide for Human Forensic Identification* (Washington, D. C., June 2005), 14.

Bibliography

U. S. Department Name. Department Office, Bureau, or Agency. *Title of Report.* Washington, D. C., Date.

U. S. Department of Justice. Office of Justice Programs. *Mass Fatality Incidents: A Guide for Human Forensic Identification.* Washington, D. C., June 2005.

INTERNET - ONLINE SOURCES

CITING INTERNET SOURCES

A detailed set of rules and conventions for identifying sources in print has been available for many years. As you can see from the previous citation samples, authors, editors, translators, and publishers are clearly identified as are the dates of publication and publisher's locations.

The Internet provides a rich field of information that is quickly and easily available. No doubt you plan to use several Internet sources for your paper. However, unlike print media, Internet sites do not have addresses in the conventional sense and cyberspace sources are frequently revised. Some may even disappear altogether.

Try to get as much bibliographic information from Web sites as possible. For example, you may not find an author or publisher. Your citation should allow your reader to get back to the site. Try to open the Web site with the citation you use. If not successful, use a different citation. The URL is usually the best.

CITING URLs AND E-MAIL ADDRESSES

Because of the possibility of transcription errors, use the edit/copy and edit/paste functions of your word processor to copy URLs and e-mail addresses directly into your paper. If you need to divide a URL between two lines, do so only after a slash (/), a double slash (//), or a colon (:). Do not divide at a hyphen - and do not add a hyphen at a break.

E-MAIL AND TEXT MESSAGES

Note

Do not include e-mail communications in your bibliography.

4. First name Last name, e-mail message to author, Date received.

4. Judy Cross, e-mail message to author, 27 November 2006.

3. Stanley Fishkoff, text message to author, 15 July 2009.

WEB SITES

Note

Include as much information as possible.

7. First name Last name or Organization Name of site creator, "Site Title," Title or Name of Page Owner, URL (accessed date).

7. National Aeronautics and Space Administration, "For Researchers," National Aeronautics and Space Administration, http://nasa.gov/audience/for researchers/features/ index.html (accessed August 1, 2007).

Bibliography

First name Last name or Organization Name of site creator. "Site Title." Title or Name of Page Owner. URL (accessed date).

National Aeronautics and Space Administration. "For Researchers." National Aeronautics and Space Administration. http://nasa. gov/audience/for researchers/features/index.html (accessed August 1, 2007).

ONLINE BOOK

Note

12. First name Last name of author, *Title.* (Publication City: Publisher, Publication Date), URL (accessed date).

12. Joseph Conrad, *Heart of Darkness.* (New York: Harper Brothers,1910), http://sunsite.berkely.edu/Literature/Conrad/ HeartofDarkness/01.html (accessed August 13, 2005).

ONLINE BOOK

Bibliography

Last name, First name. *Title.* Publication City: Publisher, Publication Date. URL (accessed date).

Conrad, Joseph. *Heart of Darkness.* New York: Harper Brothers, 1910. http://sunsite.berkely.edu/Literature/Conrad/HeartofDarkness/01.html (accessed August 13, 2005).

ARTICLE IN AN ONLINE SCHOLARLY JOURNAL

Note

1. First Name Last Name, "Article Title," *Journal Title* Volume Number (Publication Date), URL (accessed date).

1. David W. Blight, "The Slave Narrative: A Genre and A Source," *History Now* no.2 (2004), http://www.historynow.org/12_2004/historian3.html (accessed August 1, 2007).

Bibliography

Last name, First name. "Article Title." *Journal Title* Volume Number (Publication Date). URL (accessed date).

Blight, David W. "The Slave Narrative: A Genre and A Source." History Now, no. 2 (2004). http://www.historynow.org/12_2004/historian3.html (accessed August 1, 2007).

ARTICLE IN AN ONLINE MAGAZINE

Note

12. First name Last name, "Article Title," *Name of Online Magazine,* Publication Date, URL (accessed date).

12.Tony Karon, "Why Africa Has Become a Bush Priority," *Time Online Edition,* July 7, 2003, http://www.time.com/time/world/article/0,8599,463304,00.html (accessed July 14, 2003).

Bibliography

Last name, First name. "Article Title." *Name of Online Magazine,* Publication Date. URL (accessed date).

Karon, Tony. "Why Africa Has Become a Bush Priority," *Time Online Edition,* July 7, 2003. http://www.time.com/time/world/article/0,8599,463304,00.html (accessed July 14, 2004).

ARTICLE IN AN ONLINE NEWSPAPER

Note

9. First name Last name, "Article Title," ***Online Newspaper Name*****, Publication Date, URL (accessed date).**

Carl Hulse, "Democrats Fail To Force Vote on Iraq Pullout," *New York Times*, July 18, 2007, http://www.nytimes.com/2007/07/18/washington/18cnd-cong.html?hp (accessed July 18, 2007).

Bibliography

Last name, First name. "Article Title," ***Online Newspaper Name*****, Publication Date. URL (accessed date).**

Hulse, Carl, "Democrats Fail To Force Vote on Iraq Pullout," *New York Times,* July 18, 2007. http://www.nytimes.com/2007/07/18/washington/18cnd-cong.html?hp (accessed May 1, 2006).

ONLINE ENCYCLOPEDIA AND DICTIONARIES

Note

Do not include in bibliography.

8. ***Reference Book Title*****, xth ed., s.v. "Subject." URL (accessed date).**

8. *Columbia Encyclopedia,* 6th ed., s.v. "Alexander Meigs Haig." http://www.encyclopedia.com/doc/1E1-Haig-Ale.html (accessed May 1, 2006).

WEBLOGS

Note

Include as much information as possible. Do not include in bibliography unless it is significant for your paper.

7. First name Last name of blog creator, "Blog Title", Weblog name, entry posted Month Day, Year, URL (accessed date).

7. Larrry Arnstein, "New PR Plan For Archdiocese of Los Angeles," *The Huffington Post,* entry posted July 18, 2007, http://www.huffingtonpost.com/theblog/ (accessed July 18, 2007).

WEBLOGS COMMENTS

Note

Include as much information as possible. Do not include in bibliography unless it is significant for your paper. Include date of comment. If author not known or a pseudonym is used, add [*pseud.*} in brackets.

7. First name Last name of person commenting, comment on "Blog Title", Weblog name, comment posted Month Day, Year, URL (accessed date).

7. Richard Cohan, comment on "New PR Plan For Archdiocese of Los Angeles," The Huffington Post, comment posted August 15, 2007, http://www.huffingtonpost.com/theblog/ (accessed September 22, 2007).

ELECTRONIC MAILING LISTS

Note

Do not include in bibliography unless it is significant for your paper.

9. First name Last name, e-mail to Name of mailing list, Date of mailing, URL (accessed Month Day, Year).

9. Johansen, Christopher, e-mail to Exlibris mailing list, May 8, 2007, http://palimpsest.stanford.edu/byform/mailing-lists/exlibris/ (accessed August 12, 2007).

ONLINE PUBLIC DOCUMENTS

Note

Follow the format for print documents but add the URL and accessed date.

9. U. S. Department, *Document Title,* xxxth Cong., xd sess., (Washington, DC, 2004) URL (accessed date).

9. U. S. Department of the Interior, *Conservation Spending Table June 2003,* 109th Cong., 2d sess.,(Washington, DC, 2004) http://www.doi.gov/budget/index.html (accessed August 23, 2004).

Bibliography

U.S. Department of the Interior. *Conservation Spending Table June 2003.* 109th Cong., 2d sess. (Washington, DC, 2004) http://www.doi.gov/budget/index.html (accessed August 23, 2004).

TURABIAN QUOTATIONS

PROSE

Quotations of four lines or fewer are not set off from the text but are placed within double quotation marks. Quotations may be placed at the beginning, middle, or end of sentences.

Thomas Paine, in his pamphlet, *The Crisis*, wrote the stirring line, "These are the times that try men's souls."[2]

For longer quotations, use a comma after the last word of text if it is not a complete sentence or a colon if it is. Double space and type the quotation single spaced with no quotation marks. Indent same number of spaces as for paragraph indention from the left margin to begin the paragraph. The remainder of the quotation should be indented four spaces. The superscript note follows the quote.

Writing to bolster the country after the terrible first days of the war, Paine wrote,

> These are the times that try men's souls. The summer soldier and the sunshine patriot will, in this crisis, shrink from the service of their country; but he that stands it now, deserves the love and thanks of man and woman.[4]

POETRY AND DRAMA

Short quotations of two line or fewer are inserted in the text enclosed within quotation marks. If the quotation is more than one line long, the lines are separated by a slash or virgule with a space before and after.

Always the champion of those who overcame the troubles inflicted by illness or ill fortune, Henley wrote the famous lines: "I am the master of my fate: / I am the captain of my soul."

Quotations of more than two lines are centered on the page, double or single spaced, without quotation marks. The quotation, aligned on the left, should follow the format of the original as closely as possible. Set off as a block quotation like prose.

The poet wrote:

> The park is filled with night and fog,
> The veils are drawn about the world,
> The drowsy lights along the paths
> Are dim and pearled.

Poems with lines too long to be centered should be indented four spaces from the left margin with left over lines indented four more spaces.

> Long ago I learned how to sleep,
> In an old apple orchard where the wind swept
> by counting its money and throwing it away,
> In a wind-gaunt orchard where the limbs
> forked out and listened or never listened at all,

Punctuation of Quotations

Periods and commas are placed inside quotation marks. Question marks and exclamation points not originally in the quotation, are placed outside the quotation marks. Semicolons and colons go outside the quotation marks.

Quotation Within a Quotation

Use single quotation marks to set off a quotation within a quotation.

Ellipsis

When omitting words, phrases or sentences from quoted material, use three periods with a space before each and a space after the last.

Cohen's statement, "This is a war . . . that must be won." resulted in applause from both sides.

An ellipsis following a sentence has four dots. The first is the period of the first sentence.

"At first I believed that global warming was truly not a serious problem. . . . Now I have changed my belief."

An ellipsis following a sentence ending with a question mark or exclamation point has only three dots.

"How could anyone believe his ridiculous comments? . . . His arguments collapsed."

TURABIAN NUMBERS

WHEN TO USE WORDS AND NUMERALS FOR NUMBERS

Use words for all numbers from one to one hundred. Use words for numbers ending in hundred, thousand, hundred thousand, million, billion, trillion, etc.

The treasurer announced that the budget shortfall is six thousand dollars.

Use combinations of numerals and words to express very large numbers.

The local government has allocated 6.2 million for hurricane relief.

Use numerals for all other numbers.

There were 650 casualties as a result of the raid.

Use the same form for all numbers in a series. If you begin with numerals, continue with numerals even if some numbers are less than 100. If you begin with words, continue with words.

The graduating class consisted of 136 Latinos, 22 African Americans, 212 Asians, and 16 Native Americans.

Use words when a number begins a sentence. Never begin a sentence with a number.

Forty seven subjects took the first test.

Use numerals to express decimals and percentages. Spell out *percent*.

Current mortgage rates are 6 percent.

The watch costs $134.50

Use numerals when fractions and whole numbers are in the same sentence.

The birth rate rose to 1.3 from 1 per family.

Use words for fractions that stand alone.

Three fourths of the trade balance is caused by manufactured goods.

TURABIAN NUMBERS

Use numerals for parts of books.

Chapter 3 Table 7 Page 26

WHEN TO USE COMMAS IN NUMBERS

Use commas between groups of three digits in numbers above 1,000 and year dates greater than four places,

3,232,000 2,499 4,500 B.C.E.

but not after a decimal point

7,147.0631

and not after the following exceptions:

page numbers	page 1211
street addresses	**1312 Stone Street**
decimal fractions less than one	.08965

HOW TO STATE DATES, TIMES, DAYS, MONTHS, AND YEARS

Use either date month year without commas or month, date, year followed by a comma, but be consistent.

The fiercest fighting occurred on 13 June.

or

On June 13, 2006, the fiercest fighting occurred.

When only the date is stated, it is preferable to spell it out.

The date was the twenty-third of the month.

When only the month and year are stated, omit the comma.

The convention was held in January 2006.

HOW TO STATE CENTURIES

Spell in lower case century dates and hyphenate centuries with two words.

During the sixteenth century

After the twenty-first century

but hyphenate all century references that are adjectives.

eighteenth-century poetry

late twentieth-century theories

HOW TO STATE DECADES

Use either numbers with a plural s or spell out the decade.

Greenhouse gas emissions increased in the sixties.

or

During the 1960s greenhouse gas emissions increased.

HOW TO STATE MONTHS AND DAYS

Spell the names of months and days in your text.

The office will be closed during the months of June and July.

However, use abbreviations consistently in bibliographies.

Jan., Feb., Sept., Sun., Mon., Tues.

HOW TO STATE TIME

Spell the time of day except when A.M. or P.M. are used.

At 6:15 A.M. the bomb exploded.

At six o'clock in the morning the bomb exploded.

Midnight is 12:00 P.M. Noon is 12:00 M.

HOW TO USE NUMBERS DESCRIBING GOVERNMENT ORGANIZATIONS

Ordinal numbers are used to identify government groups and organizations. Spell out and capitalize numbers up to one hundred. Larger numbers use ordinal numerals.

103rd Congress   Third Reich

HOW TO STATE INCLUSIVE PAGE NUMBERS

When citing page numbers or parts of written works, cite the first page number and then only the last page number.

1007-9	491-513
300-13	11399-419
601-18	14891-902
91-6	67-71

HOW TO FORM NUMBER PLURALS

Add an s to numerals.

A cache of AK47s was found in the cave.
A fleet of Lexus ES330s were tested.

For numbers spelled out use the same form as for other nouns.

The divorce rate is highest among couples in their thirties.

The casualties numbered in the thousands.

TURABIAN CAPITALIZATION AND ITALICS

Proper Nouns

African-American   George Washington Bridge

Proper Adjectives - Adjectives derived from verbs

American   Parisian

except proper adjectives that have come into common English use.

arabic numerals euro style

WORKS

Capitalize all the words except articles, prepositions, to as part of an infinitive and conjunctions.

The War of the Roses

How to Write an Excellent Paper

SACRED TEXTS

Capitalize but do not underline, italicize, or place in quotations the titles of religious scriptures.

The Torah is the sacred book of the Jews.

The Gospel of St. Matthew opens the New Testament.

Muslims revere the Koran.

POETRY

Capitalize and italicize the titles of long poems. Capitalize and place short poems in quotation marks.

Alexander Pope's Rape of the Lock

Sandburg wrote the short poem, "Wind Song."

PLAYS - MOVIES - TELEVISION PROGRAMS

Capitalize and italicize the titles of plays, movies, radio and television programs.

PBS features Charlie Rose.

The motion picture, Capote, won five Oscar nominations.

Single episodes of a television or radio series are place in quotation marks and not italicized.

The episode "The Aircraft Carrier" of the series The Pacific War was aired 5 July 1965.

SHIPS AND AIRCRAFT

Italicize names of aircraft and ships.

USS Intrepid   Airbus 327   Queen of the Seas

FOREIGN WORDS AND EXPRESSIONS

Italicize foreign words in text that are not full quotations.

Dieu et mon droit is the motto.

But enclose the words of a full foreign quotation in quotation marks and do not italicize.

Foreign words that are in common use are not italicized.

status quo   schadenfreude   de facto

TURABIAN ABBREVIATIONS

GENERAL USE OF PERIODS

Use a period and no space after abbreviations that contain periods.

N.J.   D.Sc.   U.S.

PROPER NAMES

Use a period and a space after initials of persons.

G. K. Chesterton   R. P. Carons

Professional and Social Titles

Ms.   Mr.   Dr.

TURABIAN ABBREVIATIONS

Use abbreviations of civil, military, and religious titles with names or abbreviate titles if you prefer, but be consistent.

Sgt. Crass Admiral Smith Sen. Jones

Use abbreviations before the full name.

Dr. Richard Croner Adm. John Smith

ORGANIZATIONS

NAACP FAA CIA NFL OPEC NAFTA PGA AARP

GEOGRAPHIC NAMES

Spell geographic names within the text. In bibliographies use abbreviations such as the two letter mail forms for states.

AK NY AZ MT ID

Spell names for streets and directions in the text.

Street Court Parkway West Southeast Place

MEASURES

Spell measures under 100 with same rules as for text numbers.

300 liters twenty miles six nautical miles

100 centimeters

WRITTEN AND ARTISTIC WORKS

Spell in lower case the terms for written and art works and their parts except when in a heading or when beginning a sentence.

chapter volume section scene illustration

TURABIAN FORMATTING

PAPER

Use only high quality white paper 81/2 x 11 inches

MARGINS

In Word click on the Page Layout Tab. Click on the Margin icon. Select Normal with 1 inch margins all around.

PAGE NUMBERS

Begin numbering after the Title Page. Page numbers may be centered in the footer at the bottom of the page, centered in the header at the top, or flush right in the header. Click on the Insert Tab. Click on Page Number and Top of Page. Click on Plain Number 2 for the center position or Plain Number 3 for the flush right . For the bottom of the page click on Bottom of Page and Plain number 2.

TYPE FONT AND SIZE

Select an appropriate type face such as Times New Roman, Arial, or similar easily read type in 12 point size.

TITLE PAGE

Requirements for the title page vary. Your instructor may stipulate the requirements. In general, keep it simple. Center the title in all caps, double spaced. Type your name and the name of the course at the bottom in upper and lower case. If required, add the name of your instructor.

FIRST LINE INDENT

Click on View and Ruler. The ruler will appear at the top of the page. Move the top inverted triangle to the 1/2 inch mark on the ruler to indent the first line of each paragraph.

LINE SPACING

Regular text is double spaced. Endnotes and footnotes are single spaced. Place the cursor in a paragraph. To double space press Ctrl+2 or click on the Home Tab and Paragraph button. Select double space in the dialog box.

TURABIAN TITLE PAGE

HEALTH CARE REFORM – A UNIVERSAL HEALTH CARE SYSTEM

Mary K. O'Brian

American History 101

May 5, 2010

TURABIAN TITLE PAGE

Follow the instructions of your instructor with regard to the layout of your title page.

Health Care Reform – A Universal Health Care System

Many people believe that health care is a basic human right. Virtually everyone on the planet will contract illnesses, minor to life threatening, throughout their lives. Therefore, plans should be made for the prevention of disease to keep people healthy and for an economically sustainable program to provide care for all regardless of ability to pay. A civilized society does not allow indigents to suffer and die. Although most citizens would subscribe to these beliefs, the question before America is how to design such a health care system in a capitalist economic system.

The United States spends more on health care than anyone "but unfortunately the quality of care is going down," according to Health and Human Services Secretary Kathleen Sebelius in a conference call to reporters.[1] Many Americans who do not have private physicians use the hospital emergency rooms for even minor illnesses creating crowded conditions at great cost. Even those who have insurance frequently find that it is insufficient to cover treatments. An article in the NY Times stated that three quarters of those bankrupted by medical problems had insurance when they became ill.[2]

Unfortunately, there are competing forces in Congress. Many oppose a single payer, government financed program that would compete with private insurers. Others are concerned

---

1. Twedt, Steve. "Official: U.S. Health Costs Up, Quality Down, *Pittsburgh Post-Gazette*, June 27, 2009.

2. Albelson, Reed. "Insure, but Bankrupted by Health Crises," *New York Times*, June 30, 2009.

1

TURABIAN FIRST PAGE

Center the title at the top of the page. Double space and begin typing. Insert endnotes or footnote numbers in the text. If footnoting, type an underline one third of the way across the page after the last line of texts. Single space footnotes. Double space between footnotes. One inch margins all sides.

TURABIAN TABLES

Employer-sponsored health insurance premiums have nearly doubled since 2000, a rate three times faster than wages. In 2008, the average premium for a family plan purchased through an employer was $12,680, nearly the annual earnings of a full-time minimum wage job. Americans pay more than ever for health insurance, but get less coverage. Table1. shows the problems facing families in five selected states.

Table 1

Health Insurance Coverage in Five Selected States

States	Uninsured	Insured by Employee	Premium Cost	Increase Since 2000
NY	14%	21 million	$14,000	97%
FL	21%	9.8 million	$12,780	88%
CA	19%	19 million	$13, 297	114%
IL	14%	8.1 million	$13,631	89%

Source: United States, Dept. of Health and Human Services; Hidden Costs of Health Care, July 2009; Web; 11 Aug. 2009.

TURABIAN TABLES

Keep tables as simple as possible. Avoid using vertical rules. Type the table number flush left with an arabic numeral. Double space and type the table title capitalizing significant words.

Insert horizontal rules to separate the column heads from the table titles and the data.

Bibliography

Daschle, Thomas. *Critical: What We Can Do About the Health Care Crisis.* New York: Thomas Dunne Books, 2008.

Dranove, David. *Code Red: An Economist Explains How to Revive the Healthcare System Without Destroying It.* Princeton: Princeton University Press, 2008.

Halvorsen, George C. *Epidemic of Care: A Call for Safer, Better, and More Accountable Health Care.* San Francisco, CA: Jossey-Bass, 2003.

Kotlikoff, Laurence J. *The Healthcare Fix: Universal Insurance for All Americans.* Cambridge, MA: MIT Press, 2007.

Kronke, Charles, and Ronald White. "The Modern Health Care Maze." *Independent Review* 14, no. 1 (2009): 45-47.

Lamm, Richard. *The Brave New World of Health Care.* Golden, CO: Fulcrum Publishers, 2003.

Luft, Harold. *Total Care: The Antidote to the Health Care Crisis.* Cambridge, MA: 2008.

Newton, Michael J. *Without Your Consent: The Hijacking of American Health Care.* New Canaan, CT: Paribus Press, 2008.

O'Brien, Lawrence. *Bad Medicine: How the American Medical Establishment Is Ruining Out Health Care System.* New York: Prometheus Books, 1999.

Pressman, Aaron. "How to Play It: Health-Care Reform." *BusinessWeek,* July 6, 2009.

Reid, T. R. *The Healing of America. A Global Quest for Better, Cheaper, and Fairer Health Care.* New York: Penguin Press, 2009.

Rooney, Patrick. *America's Health Care Crisis Solved: Money-Saving Solutions, Coverage for Everyone.* Hoboken, NJ: Wiley, 2008.

Sessions, Samuel Y., and Allan S. Detsky. "Employment and US Health Care Reform. Saving Jobs While Cutting Costs." *Journal of the American Medical Association* 301, no. 17 (2009): 1811.

Twedt, Steve. "Official: U.S. Health Costs Up, Quality Down." *Pittsburgh Post-Gazette,* June 27, 2009. http://www.post-gazette.com/pg/09178/980176-28.stm#ixzz0JkSnEXQ2&D

Whitesides, John. "Congress Back To Wrestle With Healthcare Reform." *Reuters,* July 6, 2009. http://news.yahoo.com/s/nm/20090706/ts_nm/us_usa_healthcare_congress

10

TURABIAN BIBLIOGRAPHY

Label only the first page of the bibliography at the top of the page. Continue regular pagination. Double space and begin typing the bibliography. Single space within each entry but double space between entries. Use a hanging indent of about five spaces. If you used endnotes instead of footnotes, the endnote page titled, Endnotes, would precede the Bibliography page.

Part 3

Writing Review

A Writing Review

A Refresher in Mechanics, Grammar, and Usage

If you know your grammar and mechanics cold, you can skip this section. However, if you are a bit shaky in this area, you don't want to spoil all your good research work by submitting a paper with errors in mechanics, grammar, or usage. Your paper must conform to the the highest standards of usage.

This section offers you an opportunity to refresh your understanding of these language elements.

Language Mechanics

Punctuation

USE COMMAS

▶ **Before *and, but, for,* and *nor* between independent clauses.**

The judge approved the verdict, **but** the appeals court reversed it.

▶ **Between *words, phrases,* and *clauses* in series.**

We assembled ***men, women, girls,*** and ***boys.***

▶ **Between *adjectives* that modify the *same noun*.**

The flat tax will create ***new, unusual*** hardships.

▶ **To set off parenthetical comments.**

Exercising, ***however,*** is not the only way to lose weight.

▶ **To set off words which, if omitted, would not change the meaning of the sentence.**

Frank Sinatra, ***one of the most popular singers of the twentieth century,*** was a movie star.

▶ **To set off clauses beginning with *which, whom, whose, who,* and *that,* which if omitted, would not change the meaning of the sentence.**

The Boeing 747, ***which has one of the best safety records,*** was responsible for the boom in intercontinental travel.

▶ **After a long introductory clause or phrase.**

If we learn the cause of the expansion, we will be in a position to make better decisions.

USE SEMICOLONS

▶ **Between independent clauses without a conjunction.**

The men in the study were young; ***the women were old.***

▶ **To separate items in a series when the items are separated by commas.**

Speakers included ***Mr. Jones, the teacher; Ms. Crashet, the principal; and Dr. Rogers, the superintendent.***

USE COLONS

▶ **To introduce a list.**

The following members will attend the convention: ***Robertson, Bohannon, and Rabinowitz.***

▶ **To separate a complete, independent clause and a second clause that illustrates or elaborates the first. If the second is a complete sentence it begins with a capital.**

The story is a complete fabrication: ***The brothers invented the entire scenario to protect each other.***

USE DASHES

▶ **To show a sharp break in the continuity of a sentence. Use two hyphens, but use sparingly.**

Jim saw himself as handsome--***others saw him as conceited***--and played the role.

USE PARENTHESES

▶ **To show an even sharper break in the continuity of a sentence than the use of dashes.**

The New York art scene ***(for some the epitome of hypocrsy)*** is alway lively.

USE BRACKETS

▶ **To enclose a parenthesis within a parenthesis.**

(The Lenape tribe *[1710]* was part of the Iroquois group).

USE HYPHENS

Use a good dictionary as a guide, but in general use hyphens:

▶ **In compound adjectives beginning with adverbs ill, better, best, little, or well.**

better-dressed, ill-prepared, little-used, best-known, well-loved

▶ **In compound adjectives which precede a noun but not in adjectives beginning with an adverb ending in -ly.**

slow-moving vehicles, but not freshly minted money

▶ **Do not use after prefixes: after, anti, bi, counter, mid, mini, multi, non, over, pre, pro, semi, socio, sub, super, ultra, under.**

aftereffects, antifreeze, bipolar, counterattack, miniskirt, multinational, nonjudgemental, overpaid, preschool, profile, semicircular, socioeconomic, subpar, supernova, underclass

USE APOSTROPHES

▶ **To form possessive of a singular noun or a plural noun not ending in s, add an apostrophe and an s.**

Richard's thesis. *children's toys.*

▶ **To form possessive of a plural noun ending in s, add only an apostrophe.**

motorists' maps

▶ **To form the possessive of a singular proper noun, add an apostrophe and an s.**

Poe's short stories *Williams's* latest movie

▶ **To form the possessive of a plural proper noun, add only an apostrophe.**

the *Jeffersons'* family home

▶ **To form the possessive of nouns in series when the possession is shared, add an apostrophe and an s after the last noun.**

Jane, Bill, and *Rose's* office

▶ **To form the possessive of nouns in series when possession is separate, add an apostrophe and an s after each noun.**

Jane's, Bill's, and *Rose's offices*

USE PERIODS

▶ **To end a declarative or imperative sentence.**

The Russians are coming. *Face left.*

QUESTION MARKS

▶ **To end interrogative sentences.**

How is Bill feeling today?

▶ **Inside closing quotation marks if the quotation is a question.**

The teacher asked, *"What time did you finish the test?"*

▶ **Outside closing quotation marks if the whole sentence is a question.**

Why is everyone saying, "I know the answer"?

▶ **Inside closing quotation marks when it replaces a comma or period.**

"Where has everyone gone?" Mary asked.

Grammar and Usage

AGREEMENT OF SUBJECT AND VERB

A verb must agree in number and person with its subject even when phrases or clauses separate them.

Wrong:

This ***car,*** in addition to hundreds of others, ***were*** selected for export.

Correct:

This ***car,*** in addition to hundreds of others, ***was*** selected for export.

WITH INDEFINITE PRONOUNS: either, neither, everybody, everyone, somebody, and everything are singular and must agree with a singular verb.

Wrong:

Everyone of the cars ***are*** on the list.

Correct:

Everyone of the cars ***is*** on the list.

WITH COLLECTIVE NOUNS: *class, committee, assembly,* may be either singular or plural depending on whether the action takes place by a single group or the individuals within it.

Action on whole group:

The (whole) ***class was selected*** to play.

Action by individuals:

The ***class*** (members) ***are divided*** on the issue.

H PAIRED COORDINATING CONJUNCTIONS: *Neither...nor* and *either...or*

When one noun is singular and one is plural, the verb agrees with the closer noun.

Wrong:

Neither his brothers nor ***Dick were*** present.

Correct:

Neither his brothers nor ***Dick was*** present.

AGREEMENT OF PRONOUNS AND ANTECEDENTS

A pronoun must agree with its antecedent.

With Indefinite antecedent pronouns: *either, neither, everybody, everyone, somebody,* and ***everything* are singular and must be followed by singular pronouns.**

Wrong:

Everyone is looking for ***their*** books.

Correct:

Everyone is looking for ***his*** or ***her*** books.

With paired Co-ordinating Conjunctions: *neither...nor and either...or.*

When one noun is singular and one is plural, the pronoun agrees with the closer noun.

Wrong:

Neither his brothers nor ***Dick*** has ***their*** books.

Correct:

Neither his brothers nor ***Dick*** has ***his*** books.

PRONOUNS: WHO AND WHOM

Who **is a subject of a verb and *whom* is an object of a verb or preposition. An easy way to see if the use is correct is to turn the construction around and substitute *he* or *him*. If *he* fits, *who* is correct. If *him* fits, *whom* is correct. Remember, *whom* and *him* both end in the letter *m*.**

Wrong:

Who do you work for? (You work for ***he***.)

Correct:

Whom do you work for? (You work for ***him***.)

RELATIVE PRONOUNS: THAT AND WHICH

That **introduces an element which, if omitted, would change the meaning of the sentence.**

Trees ***that are green year round*** are called evergreen.

Which **introduces an element which, if omitted, would not change the meaning of the sentence.**

Trees, ***which are among nature's gifts,*** inspire me to write.

SUBORDINATE CONJUNCTIONS: BECAUSE AND SINCE

***Because* is used to indicate a causal relationship.**

The device failed ***because*** preparation was poor.

***Since* is used to indicate time.**

Since the beginning of the test period, several students have reported feeling ill.

MISPLACED MODIFIERS

Be certain modifiers are placed correctly to be sure the meaning is clear.

Bad:

The dog is for sale. He eats anything and ***loves children.***

(Does he love eating children?)

Better:

The dog is for sale. He ***loves children*** and eats anything.

Bad:

Working hard on the term paper, the teacher told John he was doing well. (Who is working on the term paper?)

Better:

Working hard on the term paper, John was praised by his teacher.

PARALLEL CONSTRUCTION

Be sure that all sentence elements which express parallel ideas are in the same form.

After coordinating conjunctions: *and, but, or,* and *nor*

Wrong:

The author concluded that gross ***sales*** had improved but the individual ***stores*** had not. (comparing sales with stores)

Correct:

The author concluded that gross ***sales*** had improved, but that individual store's ***sales*** had not.

With paired coordinating conjunctions: *not only...but also, both...and, either...or, neither...nor, between...and*

▶ **both ...and**

Wrong:

The courses advertised were both ***interesting*** and ***of great difficulty***.

(present participle and prepositional phrase)

Correct:

The courses advertised were both ***of great interest*** and ***of great difficulty***.

(two prepostional phrases)

▶ **not only...but also**

Wrong:

Members were ***not only upset*** with the vote, ***but also they resented*** the officious manner of the president.

(single adjective and independent clause)

Correct:

Members were ***not only upset*** with the vote, but ***also resentful*** of the officious manner of the president.

(adjective and adjective)

▶ **neither...nor and either...or**

Wrong:

Neither the ***girls' scores*** on the first trial ***nor*** the ***scores of the boys*** were correctly recorded.

(adjective modifying noun and prepositional phrase modifying noun)

Correct:

Neither the ***girls' scores*** on the first trial ***nor*** the ***boys' scores*** were correctly recorded.

(adjective modifying noun and adjective modifying noun)

Between...and

Wrong:

The difference ***between*** the ***ideas*** of the world leaders ***and*** the local ***politicians*** is apparent.

(noun-ideas and noun-people)

Correct:

The difference ***between*** the ***ideas*** of the world leaders ***and*** the ***opinions*** of the local politicians is apparent.

(noun-ideas and noun-opinions)

Among elements in series

Wrong:

They were asked ***to return early, to clean the site,*** and ***that the group begin the new work.***

(two infinitive phrases and a subordinate clause)

Correct:

They were asked ***to return early, to clean the site,*** and ***to begin work.***

(three infinitive phrases)

Index

About the Author

Alvin Baron has had a distinguished career in education. Beginning in New York City in an elementary school in the Bedford-Stuyvesant neighborhood, he later taught English and language arts at Whitelaw Reid Junior High School and Lafayette High School in Brooklyn. After teaching for many years, he was appointed to the position of assistant principal of McKinley Junior HIgh School and later principal of P.S. 274, a large inner city elementary school.

He continued his career in school administration as principal of the suburban Lawrence Junior High School in Long Island, New York, and later assumed the leadership of the Lawrence High School. He was selected as Superintendent of the Lawrence Public Schools which he led for many years before appointments as superintendent in Franklin Square and Port Washington.

Dr. Baron earned bachelor's and master's degrees from Brooklyn College and was awarded the Doctor of Philosophy degree from New York University. He has taught at New York University, City University of New York, and Hofstra University.

His love of teaching inspired him to begin writing books that would encourage students to love language and excel in their own writing. His books have been published in many editions, each surpassing the last in popularity. He now devotes full time to writing and helping students with research projects.

Dr. Baron believes the Internet will surpass the printing press in its impact on world civilization and he continuously updates his books to include the latest advances in using this amazing tool to help scholars find and use information.

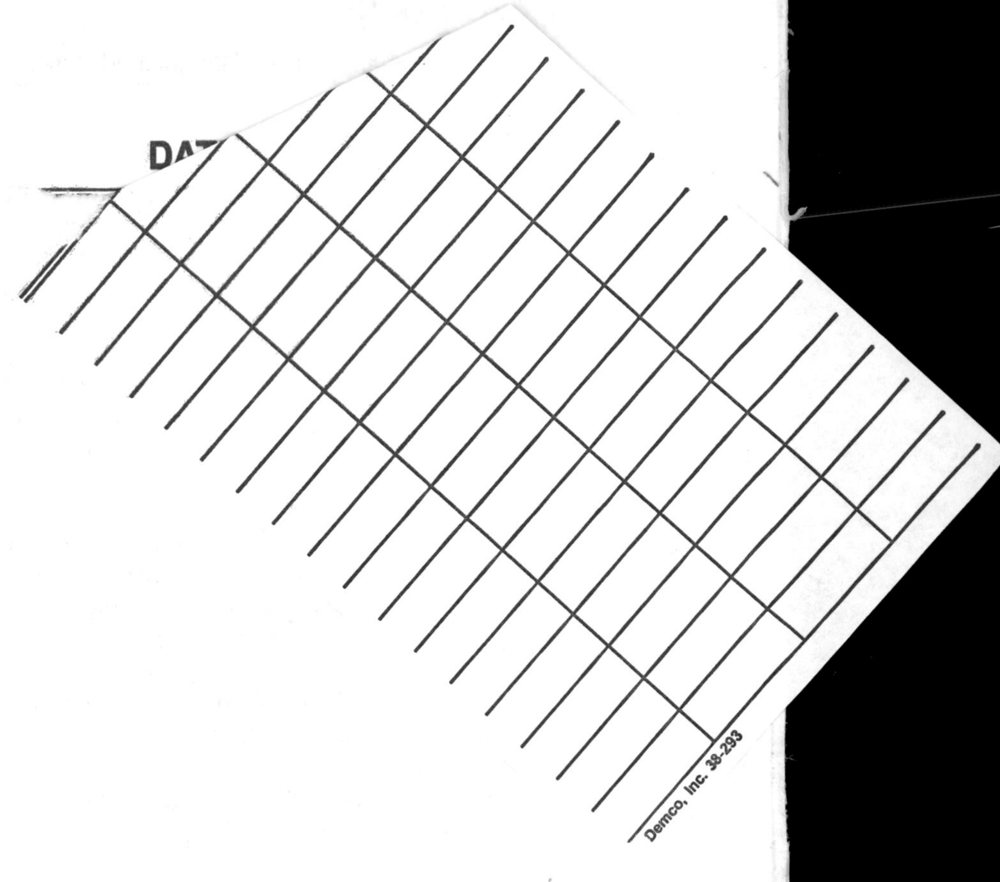
DAT
Demco, Inc. 38-293